NOAH WEBSTER *1758-1843*

ON BEING AMERICAN
Selected Writings, 1783–1828

68

Noah Webster at age
sixty-five. Engraved by
A. B. Durand from
an original portrait by
Samuel F. B. Morse and
used as frontispiece for
the first edition of *An
American Dictionary of
the English Language.*

NOAH WEBSTER

ON BEING AMERICAN

Selected Writings, 1783–1828

EDITED AND WITH AN INTRODUCTION BY
HOMER D. BABBIDGE, JR.

FREDERICK A. PRAEGER, *Publishers*
New York • Washington • London

FREDERICK A. PRAEGER, PUBLISHERS
111 Fourth Avenue, New York, N.Y. 10003, U.S.A.
77–79 Charlotte Street, London W.1, England

Published in the United States of America in 1967
by Frederick A. Praeger, Publishers

© 1967 by Homer D. Babbidge, Jr.

Library of Congress Catalog Card Number: 67–20496

PICTURE CREDITS:
Frontispiece, courtesy of the Massachusetts Historical Society; page
16, the American Antiquarian Society; pages 46 and 74, courtesy of
the New York Public Library.

Printed in the United States of America

TO
ALLALIE
AND
ALLALEE

Contents

List of Illustrations

NOAH WEBSTER *1758-1843*

ON BEING AMERICAN
Selected Writings, 1783–1828

AN EDITORIAL NOTE

An effort has been made, in editing the essays of Noah Webster, to preserve the original spelling and punctuation. Changes have been made only where the original might have led to confusion or misunderstanding for a modern reader or where, in the opinion of the editor, the original text included an apparent misspelling or typographical error. Those familiar with the work of Webster will appreciate the difficulty of such decisions.

H.D.B., Jr.

INTRODUCTION

The altogether human habit that leads us to identify a man by a single personal trait or physical attribute—to remember a Benedict Arnold for his treachery alone—has for more than a century categorized one of America's most illustrious and many-faceted historical figures as "the man who made the dictionary." The great *An American Dictionary of the English Language* stands today as a monument to Noah Webster, but the full dimensions of his career have been obscured in its shadow.

Such a truncated reputation does Webster a grave injustice, for in terms of vision, ability, dedication, and versatility, he deserves a place among that extraordinary group of men known to us today as founders of the American nation. Webster was a prominent author, editor, and publicist long before he began work on his famous dictionary; indeed, had it not been for that astonishing accomplishment, he might be better known to us today as a striking representative of early American nationalistic thought. A brief list of claims made in his behalf by those who have looked beyond the curtain of his lexicographic success suggests the dimensions of his career. He has been called "Schoolmaster to America," "the Man Who Taught the Masses How To Read and Write," "the Father of American Copyright Law," "the First Historian of Epidemic Disease," and "the Colossus of the Federalists." He was a founder of the Connecticut Academy of Arts and Sciences, Amherst College, and what was perhaps the first philological society in America. He held a variety of public offices—from judge to legislator—in both Connecticut and Massachusetts, and worked, throughout the eighty-five years of his life, as a schoolteacher, magazine and newspaper editor and publisher, lawyer, lecturer, farmer, author, and essayist. In breadth of interest and accomplishment, Webster had few superiors in the glittering Age of American En-

3

lightenment. Though a certain humorless rigidity of character and manner—his detractors called him "the Monarch"—denied Webster the role in national politics he might otherwise have enjoyed, he made vital contributions to the emergence of the American nation, both politically and culturally. But these prior accomplishments disappeared from the public consciousness, like so many sandpiper tracks from the ocean shore, under the wave of fame that followed on the publication, in 1828, of *An American Dictionary of the English Language*. So dramatic was this culminating event in his career that its earlier acts and scenes have been forgotten.

It is not my intention to delineate the full career of Noah Webster in this volume, but rather to call attention to a remarkably consistent theme in the man's literary efforts and to bring together, in one place, a representative collection of his extraordinary contributions to the literature of American patriotism. While the selections assembled here do hint at the range of the author's interests, they are intended principally to document Webster's dominant sense of purpose throughout his long and active life.

In a sense, Noah Webster's career had two distinct acts. The first—and most appealing, from hindsight—was his career as a militant advocate of American union and cultural and political independence. For fifteen years, from 1782 to 1797, Webster toiled with enthusiasm and dedication to instill in the hearts and minds of his fellow citizens some of his own passionate love of liberty and to persuade them of the great truth of his life, that liberty could be preserved only through the strength that comes of unity. Webster's career as a "cultural nationalist" entitles him to unchallenged eminence in American life, for his broadly conceived ideal of union and its cultural dimensions surpasses that of his more famous contemporaries.

The second act of Webster's career only partly negated the first. In it, he emerges not so much as an individual proponent of national unity, but as a classic symbol of the lost cause of American Federalism. Disillusioned by what he considered the demoralization of American politics, Webster turned, with the century, from political activism to moral criticism, his shining vision of the new America tarnished. With increasing piety and diminishing humanness, Webster moved away from the affairs of men to the pursuits of the mind and the spirit. He became, in his later years, the very model of the irascible, crotchety conservative, looking with equal disdain upon the folly of his youth and its reflection in nineteenth-century democratic practice.

Bred of stolid Connecticut Puritan stock, nurtured in the stern Calvinism of the eighteenth century, and educated at the orthodox little college at New Haven, the Webster of provincial, propertied, and pious loyalties seems a perfectly natural product of his environment. That he should have played an important role in organizing the Hartford Convention of 1814—because the federal government did not adequately reflect the *"northern* or *commercial* interest"[1]—seems more natural than his statement, in 1785, that "the interest of individuals must always give place to the interest of the whole community." (See Selection Two, p. 34.)

Webster's early devotion to revolutionary ideals can be attributed to exposure during his youth to the contagious spirit of political independence then abroad in New England and, more particularly, to the especially potent form of the virus that affected Yale College while he was there. His intense devotion to these ideals indicates the extraordinary grip this radical spirit had on the mind of Yale's wartime generation.

Professor David Potter discusses the role of Yale College as a seedbed not only of independence but also of union among the American colonies.[2] He quite properly cites the farewell address of Timothy Dwight as a high-water mark in the tide of sentiment that caused the class of 1769 to appear at graduation "wholly dressed in the manufactures of our own country." To Dwight, a young tutor at the college during Webster's undergraduate career, must go considerable credit for Webster's infection with these advanced ideals.

Webster derived from his career at Yale an exciting concept of American nationality and destiny—the concept of a nation that John Trumbull of the class of 1768 described as "the first in letters as the first in arms." The cultural baptism he received in the atmosphere there during the Revolutionary War, including an undergraduate glimpse of the great George Washington and an uncomfortable, but perfectly safe, march to join in the Battle of Saratoga, confirmed Webster as a patriot in the broadest sense of his own definition. Before he had reached his majority, Webster saw the visions of liberty and union as two sides of the same political and cultural coin.

Once out of Yale, however, Webster had some difficulty finding the right medium for the expression of his sentiments. He tried his hand at schoolteaching, taking time out when he could afford it to study law. By the time his first book appeared in 1783, he had been admitted to the Connecticut bar and had satisfied himself that schoolmastering was not a sufficient outlet for his growing ambitions. In his famous *The American Spelling Book* (Part I of *A Grammatical Institute of the English Language*), Webster sought to "promote the honour and prosperity" of America by establishing American independence in this rudimentary branch of literature. Encouraged by public response, he ventured to take a more prominent place in public affairs. Returning

---

[1] Letter to Oliver Wolcott, May 13, 1808, in Emily Ellsworth Fowler Ford, *Notes on the Life of Noah Webster*, ed. Emily Ellsworth Ford Skeel (New York: privately printed, 1912), II, 36.

[2] David M. Potter, "Nathan Hale and the Ideal of American Union," *Connecticut Antiquarian*, VI, No. 1 (June, 1954), pp. 20–26.

to his native Hartford, he peppered the Connecticut *Courant*[3] with anonymous letters on a variety of political and economic subjects and, in 1785, published his *Sketches of American Policy*. This slender volume, revealing Webster's considerable debt to Rousseau and other contemporary democratic writers, contained a plea for strong national government, which Madison was later to acknowledge as an "early" expression of the sentiment that culminated in the Constitution of 1787.[4] Believing that no one else had yet formulated such clear views on the need for a strong central government, Webster gave them wide play during an extensive lecture tour through the colonies in 1785–86. As a result of this tour—on which Webster promoted both the adoption of copyright laws and the sale of his book—his views on language matured. Taken together, the preface to Webster's *A Grammatical Institute of the English Language*, his *Sketches of American Policy*, and his *Dissertations on the English Language* (not published until 1789) represent a comprehensive statement of the cultural nationalism that Webster was determined to promulgate.

Webster's nationalism had two essential characteristics, remarkable not so much for their novelty as for their directness and simplicity. First, it embodied the familiar conviction that only in union was there sufficient strength to ensure liberty. In that sense, Webster shared the characteristic of all the great leaders of American independence, "the whole-heartedness with which they embraced the ideal of Union as well as the ideal of Freedom."[5] Of the local, colonial liberty that existed under the Articles of Confederation, Webster cried in 1787, "From such liberty, O Lord, deliver us!" (See Selection Three, p. 52.) He saw in the inability of the national government to enforce its policies "a ridiculous farce, a burlesque on government, and a re-proach to America," because it permitted individual states to negate common policy and gave America no effectual protection against alien intrusion. (See Selection Two, p. 41.)

The second feature of Webster's nationalism was inextricably bound up with his devotion to political union. He believed that a sense of nationality was vital to the preservation of unity, just as union was essential to liberty. Of political affairs he observed, "We ought to generalize our ideas and our measures. We ought not to consider our-selves as inhabitants of a particular state only, but as *Americans*, as the common subjects of a great empire." (See Selection Two, p. 44.) Nor was this concept of nationality limited to his adage that selfishness is "self-ruin, and that *provincial interest* is inseperable from *national*

[3] For an interesting account of Webster's relationship with the *Courant*, see Bob Eddy, "The *Courant* Took a Chance," *The Quill*, LII, No. 5 (May, 1964), pp. 12–15.

[4] See the Introduction to *Sketches of American Policy*, ed. Harry R. Warfel (New York: Scholars' Facsimiles & Reprints, 1937).

[5] Potter, *op. cit.*, p. 22.

interest." (See Selection Two, p. 45.) Webster saw Americanism as something intimately tied up with everyday matters of dress, speech, manners, and education; he argued that a true spirit of nationality could develop only from a sense of distinctiveness in the personal, daily life of the people. Cultural independence was the mortar for the stones of political union, just as union was the foundation of liberty.

Conspicuous by its absence from Webster's thinking was that spirit of egalitarian democracy and humanitarianism that had characterized the nationalism of contemporary French thinkers and that subsequently became a vital part of American national purpose. As radical as his views were in the context of his background, Webster, even in his earliest political essays, cautioned against the kind of direct democracy that had prevailed in early Greece, where an "illiterate and credulous" people "under no restraint" had provided "capricious and irregular" government. He advocated, instead, a representative democracy held in check by a strong constitution vigorously enforced. He saw property ownership as the real source of power in society and felt that the general distribution of property in America assured that civil power would remain with the people. He saw as the great task facing America the creation of a constitution, a set of laws, and a system of education that would constructively harness the popular will and provide effective protection for the rights of person and property. Believing that "the privileges of freemen are interwoven into the very feelings and habits of the Americans," he concerned himself politically with the ways and means of institutionalizing liberty. (See Selection Three, p. 58.) In this respect he was more an objective political scientist than a militant advocate of democratic institutions, more a protector than a promoter of democracy.

Qualifications on Webster's debt to the egalitarians are apparent also in his efforts against slavery. Though offended by the "injustice" of slavery and active in founding one of the nation's first abolitionist societies, the Connecticut Society for the Promotion of Freedom and the Relief of Persons unlawfully holden in Bondage, Webster in his *Effects of Slavery on Morals and Industry* (1793) concerns himself with the harmful economic and social effects of slavery, rather than with its offenses against mankind. His gradualist approach to emancipation and his preoccupation with the dollars-and-cents value of freeing the slaves suggest that Webster was not a passionate humanitarian. No matter what spirit later generations might choose to infuse into their institutions, Webster's objective was to secure for them the freedom to make that choice. Such freedom, he believed, could be obtained only through the development of union, both political and cultural.

Webster devoted his prodigiously active career from 1783 to 1800 to the task of developing a spirit of American nationality. On the political front, he served as a publicist for the new Constitution (1787–

88). In 1793, he founded the daily *American Minerva* (later renamed
the *Commercial Advertiser*) in New York and worked assiduously as its
editor until 1798, to promote the policies—notably neutrality—of
Washington's administration. Although considered a spokesman for
such leading Federalists as Jay and Hamilton (both of whom had encouraged the establishment of the newspaper), Webster felt that his
tireless efforts were nonpartisan and constructive and that his single
enemy was "disunion," the only "really formidable" threat to
America.[6] In these journalistic efforts he did much to promote the
figure of Washington as a symbol of Americanism, as well as to defend
the policies of his administration. Webster composed pamphlets stressing
the economic advantages and cultural importance of political union; he
wrote one of the first comprehensive histories of the Revolutionary
War, gave wide circulation to the addresses of Revolutionary thinkers,
and otherwise helped to build a nucleus of American folklore on which
he and others could begin to elaborate a sense of American being.

Webster paid particular attention to the more intimate aspects of
national character. Worthy of the fame it brought him was his development of the concept of an American language—a modified usage by
means of which Americans would be distinguishable from their English
forebears. Throughout his long and varied career, from the "Blue-
Backed Speller" to the great Dictionary, this was the dominant chord
in the nationalistic score of Webster's life. Long after political disillusionment had robbed him of his enthusiasm for democracy and for
the government that fostered it, the aged Webster could devote himself to the cause of a national language with the full measure of his
patriotism. In this work Webster was an effective publicist. He pointed
a schoolmasterly finger of shame at his fellow citizens for their dependence on European and English standards in speech, as well as
manners and dress. Incessantly, he appealed to their self-respect, accusing them of lack of character in failing to make their own independent
way through life. He capitalized on a lingering hostility toward the
British in order to accomplish his ends and at times took advantage of
American ignorance of Europe to caricature and attack its manners
and morals. His ability to marshal economic, social, political, and moral
arguments in a way that appealed to a wide range of Americans was
impressive. He could accentuate the positive by extolling the future
glory of America, and he could frighten Americans by describing the
untold evils in store for American youth in the dens of European de-
bauchery. He sold abolition on economic grounds and made opposition
to simplified spelling smack of treason. He could be moralistic, even
sanctimonious, or he could be bitter and vituperative. All things were
fair for Webster in his private war to create an American spirit, for
he divined that without the spirit, the union was lost; and without
the union, liberty was lost.

[6] Ford, *Notes on the Life of Noah Webster*, I, 454.

Always, however, the dominant note in Webster's writing was an appeal to that germ of nationalistic sentiment that lingered from the Revolution, when a pressing common cause had excited a sense of national identity among the thirteen colonies. For example, in appealing for the adoption of an American system of education, Webster stated, "But every child in America should be acquainted with his own country. He should read books that furnish him with ideas that will be useful to him in life and practice. As soon as he opens his lips . . . he should lisp the praises of liberty and of those illustrious heroes and statesmen who have wrought a revolution in his favor." (See Selection Five, p. 84.)

Thus did Webster attempt to tease the Revolutionary spirit of Americans out into broader fields and to diffuse it through the customs and institutions of the new country. Throughout his life he directed special attention to American education, partly because the youth of America had not been exposed firsthand to the glorious spirit of '76 and partly because he believed that "the only practicable method to reform mankind is to begin with children." (See Selection Five, p. 83.) He agreed with Montesquieu that educational practice should be related to the political principles of a nation, and he argued forcefully for an indigenous American system of education. One of the first American educators to recognize the unique function of education in a republican form of government, Webster endeavored in his extensive series of schoolbooks to acquaint young Americans with the political history of their country in general and its political institutions in particular. His "Federal Catechism," included in *An American Selection of Lessons in Reading and Speaking*, suggests the religiosity of Webster's devotion to this objective, and his later opinion that Americans were as advanced as Europeans in their study and knowledge of politics undoubtedly served to justify the importance he attached to such study.

That Webster had an economic interest in the extension of patriotic sentiment, insofar as it prompted the sale of books that were based on this kind of appeal, cannot be disregarded. He worked hard to win endorsement for his schoolbooks and to promote their sale, just as he labored for a body of copyright law that would ensure an income from these sales. But Webster's career is studded with too many economically unprofitable acts of patriotism to justify a belief that he promoted nationalism merely to sell his books. While Webster did create a demand for his own books, he performed the same service for many other authors whose profits exceeded the meager royalties that he realized on most of his works. Moreover, his interest in Americanism outlasted his concern for royalties. Long after the Revolutionary spirit had waned, he reissued *An American Selection of Lessons in Reading and Speaking* "to instruct our youth in what belongs to this country."[7]

---

[7] Quoted in Harry R. Warfel, *Noah Webster: Schoolmaster to America* (New York: The Macmillan Co., 1936), p. 90.

What is perhaps more impressive, the doughty schoolmaster dared to do what few authors in his limited circumstances would: He withdrew one of his books from the market "on the ground of . . . imperfections," an act described by a biographer as "a precious example of integrity."[8]

Webster's varied activities in the promotion of American nationalism attracted the abuse and ridicule so characteristic of the period. Republican partisans considered him a virtual monarchist, and the reactionary William Cobbett called him a "toad in the service of sans-culottism."[9] Though this criticism may be taken as evidence of Webster's effectiveness, his sensitivity to it was partly responsible for his temporary retirement from public life, in 1789, when he wrote President Washington, "I wish now to attend solely to my profession and to be unknown in any other sphere of life."[10] It was a factor, too, in Webster's final retirement from the role of publicist, in 1798, when he announced his intention to "pursue, with little interruption, my taste for science."[11] His withdrawal to New Haven in 1798, an act of great significance in Webster's life, was a symbolic retirement to the sidelines of national affairs and marked the beginning of the career that made him famous. His political comments thereafter, though frequent and militant, served only to emphasize his failure to follow in the flood of democratic sentiment that was sweeping America.

Disenchanted by the sober study of the French Revolution he had made for the *American Minerva* and alarmed by the similarity between the mushrooming democratic clubs and the despised Jacobins, Webster showed signs of losing faith in the government he had helped to create. Never an egalitarian, and always a staunch advocate of property as the basis of franchise, Webster now saw control of what was to have been the glorious new America falling into the hands of the ignorant, emotional rabble. He saw in equal suffrage a "monstrous inversion of the natural order of society" and in the ability of people without property to tax those who had accumulated it a "species of oppression that will ultimately produce a revolution."[12] A ringing Federalist victory in the Connecticut elections of 1798 was momentarily reassuring, but he cautioned a Fourth of July audience that year to proceed with care, observing that "*Experience* is a safe pilot, but *experiment* is a dangerous ocean, full of rocks and shoals."[13]

In this new role, Webster became a virtual prototype of the disillusioned Federalist. He still believed in liberty—individual and col-

---

[8] *Ibid.*, p. 306.

[9] *Ibid.*, p. 234.

[10] September 2, 1790, in *Letters of Noah Webster*, ed. H. R. Warfel (New York: Library Publishers, 1953), p. 86.

[11] Letter to Timothy Pickering, April 13, 1798, in Ford, *Notes on the Life of Noah Webster*, I, 434.

[12] Fourth of July Address, New Haven, 1802.

[13] Fourth of July Address, New Haven, 1798.

lective—and in the union that made it possible. "Man is too feeble to protect himself," he said in 1802, "and unless he can protect himself, he is not free."[14] What alarmed him was the susceptibility of the people, who, he believed, were putting into office a group of self-seeking, corrupt, and immoral men. Webster's essential confidence in the people had been based on the "substantial yeomanry" that he saw about him in Connecticut—these being moderately well educated and, in large part, property-owning. Immigration, population increases, and a more complex economy could only detract from that confidence, which had never been unlimited. On the eve of a period that posterity would one day call the zenith of democracy and the nadir of education, Webster saw the people re-enacting the tragedy of early Greece, where a similar populace had been "generally at the command of some noisy demagogue." He attacked Jefferson and "partisans" on both sides for exciting the passions of the people and urged that the people be given an opportunity to contemplate the "pernicious effects" of "hasty councils," for he remained essentially confident that "it is morally impossible that the body of a people can be enemies to public happiness."

He longed for a government "where *constitution* and *law* and *wisdom* have the control,"[15] instead of the popular democracy of Jefferson and his followers. So strong was his belief in representative constitutional government that the first evidence of partisan popular rule—especially the spoils system—left him stunned and horrified. At first, Webster clung to the view that courageous, enlightened leadership could remedy the situation; thus, he charged the Federalist leaders with attempting "to resist the force of current popular opinion instead of falling into the current with a view to direct it."[16] But he, too, eventually pulled himself up onto the bank when it became apparent that he could do nothing but be drowned in that current. In the pious quietude of his old age, Webster would one day yearn for a community to which he could remove himself "to be freed from our democracy." "We deserve all our public evils," he said. "We are a degenerate and wicked people. That a kind Providence may watch over . . . all of us is [my] prayer."[17]

Disillusioned as he was by what the American people chose to make of their freedom despite his warnings, Webster did not surrender his desire to promote a sense of Americanism among them. He observed in 1800 that "nothing like a well-defined national character" existed outside New England,[18] and he sought new outlets for the expression of his patriotic values and new means for their dissemination throughout

[14] Fourth of July Address, New Haven, 1802.
[15] Quoted in Warfel, *Noah Webster: Schoolmaster to America*, p. 425.
[16] Letter to Rufus King, July 6, 1807, in Warfel, *Letters of Noah Webster*, p. 277.
[17] Quoted in Warfel, *Noah Webster: Schoolmaster to America*, p. 425.
[18] *Ten Letters to Dr. Priestley* (1800), p. 25.

the United States. He found these in what he called "literary pursuits," which "afford the highest satisfaction without the vexations, disappointments, and endless perturbations" that he had encountered in the arena of public affairs.[19]

After his withdrawal from public affairs, Webster took two steps that fixed the course of his life thereafter: He gave himself to the church and he devoted his talents almost exclusively to the elevation of American science and letters. Webster may have felt that his contributions here would ultimately have beneficial political effects on the people, but he also believed that there was intrinsic value in the two labors of his later life—the extension of religious morality and the elevation and general diffusion of learning. Of Timothy Dwight's line, "Be freedom, and science, and virtue, thy fame," Webster was, despite his conservatism, able to salvage two-thirds. His formal commitment to virtue took place in the winter of 1807–8, when he publicly espoused the "moderate Calvinist" Church, though he recalled that a reading of Samuel Johnson's *Rambler* had led him in his youth to "a firm resolution to pursue a course of virtue through life, and to perform all moral and social duties with scrupulous exactness." The transformation that took place in 1808 was a repudiation of his earlier "mistake" of "attending to the duties which man owes to man," while neglecting those he owed "to our Creator and Redeemer."[20] That this new view of virtue was to intrude at times upon his personal and literary life was immediately evident, for on October 13, 1808, he wrote his classmate and friend Joel Barlow explaining why he could not, as he had intended, write a public review of the latter's *Columbiad:* "Of the poem as a poem I can conscientiously say all, perhaps, which you can expect or desire, but I cannot in a review omit to pass a severe censure on the atheistical principles it contains."[21]

Webster was to express his thanks for divine favor frequently thereafter, for his new-found religious faith was an indispensable support to him in the greatest labor of his life. At the same time, however, his religious orientation led him increasingly to a moral view of political affairs that made it difficult for him to recall the realities of the political world. The one word that Webster actually created—to describe the effects of the French Revolution—was defined in his great dictionary as follows:

DEMORALIZE—To corrupt or undermine the morals of; to destroy or lessen the effect of moral principles on; to render corrupt in morals.

[19] Letter to Rufus King, July 6, 1807, in Warfel, *Letters of Noah Webster,* p. 277.

[20] Letter to Thomas Dawes, December 20, 1808, in Ford, *Notes on the Life of Noah Webster,* II, 42.

[21] Quoted in Warfel, *Letters of Noah Webster,* pp. 308–9.

So convinced was Webster of the essential morality of his own position that he fell into the error of assuming the absence of morality in the views of those who opposed him. Over and over again he was to bemoan the demoralization of American government. Webster devoted considerable energy during the remaining thirty-five years of his life to the promotion of religious morality, in and out of politics. His revision of the Bible in 1833 and his central role in the founding of Amherst College in 1820 "for the education of pious young men for the gospel ministry" attest to the force of his conviction and are in contrast to its less constructive applications in the area of politics.

Webster's abundant energies, stimulated by a renewed sense of moral responsibility but frustrated in the channels of political life, poured with steady force into the riverbed of his literary course. It seems doubtful that Webster could have completed the 1828 dictionary had not his sentiments ruled out continued extensive participation in political affairs and allowed him to concentrate all his energy, ambition, and public spirit on the single goal of promoting the intellectual dignity of America.

Webster's first major undertaking after his withdrawal from New York, the preparation of *A Brief History of Epidemic and Pestilential Diseases,* was one of the most impressive scientific labors to emerge from the young nation and convincingly demonstrated that Webster was determined to make a mark for American science. Though since proven wrong in its speculations on the causes of epidemic diseases, the work is a bench mark of careful historical research, and the labor that produced it was excellent preparation for the mammoth work Webster was to undertake next.

According to his own accounts, Webster's formal venture into lexicography began at the turn of the century. The germ of the idea having been planted some years before, Webster had begun to make marginal notes of errors, new usages, and unfamiliar words in his extensive reading during his active editorial career, in subconscious preparation for his first formal effort at defining words. The motivation for the work, however, had been with him from his youth, when in the course of his early lectures he began to develop his views on "Reasons why the English should not be our Standard, either in Language or Manners."[22] His earliest literary research led him to find fault with the work of Robert Lowth and Samuel Johnson, two great standards of the day, and he began at once to plant his explosive nationalist spirit in whatever faults he could find. Webster delighted in detonating his charges in print and conducted a systematic campaign to crack the walls of English convention even before he began the constructive effort of his great dictionary. His extensive research during the first quarter of the nineteenth century only added to his enthusiasm, and by 1816, when challenged by John Pickering for his lack of respect for English literary

[22] A Syllabus of Mr. Webster's Lectures on the English Language and on Education" (1786).

authority, Webster gave free run to his sentiments. His philological and etymological studies had, he told Pickering, led him to "withdraw much of . . . [his] confidence" in the great English writers and had made him "look with astonishment upon the errors and false principles which they have propagated." (See Selection Ten, p. 150.) He leveled criticism at Johnson over and over again, as he had in an open letter to Judge Dawes on July 25, 1809, in which he stated that "the definitions which constitute the whole value of *Johnson's* Dictionary are deficient in precision beyond anything I could have imagined."[23]

Webster knew well that such criticism rang hollow without a better dictionary to replace the one he challenged. Faultfinding had come easily to one whose entire career had been devoted to breaking the "charm of veneration" of foreign authorities. Providing the constructive alternative was a backbreaking labor, but its successful completion properly earned for its executor the eternal regard of his country. A quarter-century of persistent work, "beating the track of the alphabet with sluggish resolution" (as Johnson saw the lexicographer's task), years of study in dozens of languages, the construction of an extensive theory of etymology, an extended trip to Europe, and the writing *by hand* of more than seventy thousand entries—these were the chief, though far from sole, occupations of Webster between the ages of forty-two and seventy. When, with trembling hand, Webster completed the last entry in his manuscript, he had forged the most impressive link in that "band of national union" that had been the single object of his career. He had given America its own independent standard of language—one that was good enough to become, in a few short years, the standard of the English-speaking world. Thus did Webster, by diverting his nationalist spirit into the remote channel of literary scholarship, make his greatest single contribution to the elusive object of his life. He had fulfilled, in part, his prediction of an earlier year that "We shall realize a new species of independence—an independence flattering to generous minds, and more productive of wealth than all the laws of power or the little arts of national policy."[24]

His devotion to Washingtonian policies, his abhorrence of political parties, his attachment to property and commerce, his tendency to equate New England values and interests with those of the nation, and his ultimate political disillusionment made Noah Webster a brilliant personification of "Steady Habit" Federalism. But when political disenchantment came and he found the times intolerant of his antique views, Webster defied the prototype. He largely resisted the tendency of the old-line Federalists to abandon their original confidence in the destiny of America; instead, he funneled his energies into constructive literary channels.

[23] *Columbian Centennial* (Boston), August 2, 1809, quoted in Ford, *Notes on the Life of Noah Webster*, II, 65.
[24] *An American Selection of Lessons in Reading and Speaking* (1787).

The thread of patriotism in the varied pattern of Webster's life thus sustained itself in political disillusion. From that day in 1782, when, with "the American army . . . lying on the bank of the Hudson" and with "no certain prospect of peace," he undertook his first book "to promote the honour and prosperity of . . . America," to the climactic achievement of his great dictionary in 1828, which he presented to the public with wishes "for the glory of my country," Webster's life was dedicated to the ideals of American liberty and union. For this, despite his ultimately unpopular political views, posterity must rank Noah Webster as one of America's most devoted patriots.

The genius of Webster's contribution to America's self-image was his recognition that union is built not of laws and policies or of economic and political advantage alone, but of all of these welded together by the spirit and symbols of national self-consciousness. His life was a combination of breadth of conception and interest, as reflected in his extraordinary range of writings, and a marked singleness of purpose. Politics was only one important expression of the varied media through which he tried to promote that single object—the creation of a free and unified America. His writings on history, geography, science, and simplified spelling, though less important, were similar links in the chain of unity he tried to forge during his lifetime. And the two great monuments of his career—the "Blue-Backed Speller" and *An American Dictionary of the English Language*—though they stand as the most important evidence of Webster's work, are nonetheless only parts of that same unity.

FABLE I. *Of the Boy that stole Apples.*

AN old man found a rude boy upon one of his trees stealing apples, and desired him to come down; but the young sauce-box told him plainly he would not. Won't you, said the old man, then I will fetch you down; so he pulled up some tufts of grass, and threw at him; but this only made the youngster laugh, to think the old man should pretend to beat him out of the tree with grass only.

Well, well, said the old man, if neither words nor grass will do, I must try what virtue there is in stones; so the old man pelted him heartily with stones; which soon made the young chap hasten down from the tree, and beg the old man's pardon.

M O R A L.

If good words and gentle means will not reclaim the wicked, they must be dealt with in a more severe manner.

H

A page from the 1783 edition
of the spelling book showing one of
Webster's illustrated fables.

"American Glory Begins to Dawn . . ."

From the Introduction to *The American Spelling Book*, Part I of
A Grammatical Institute of the English Language, 1783

EDITOR'S COMMENTS

"In the year 1782, while the American army was lying on the bank of the Hudson, I kept a classical school in Goshen, Orange County, State of New York. I there compiled two small elementary books for teaching the English language." Thus did Noah Webster record the origin of one of the most influential volumes in the annals of publishing. The first part of *A Grammatical Institute of the English Language,* known later as *The American Spelling Book*—and, more affectionately, as the "Blue-Backed Speller"—has had an extraordinary publishing history. Inadequate records, compounded by the then current practice of "pirating" editions, make it impossible to confirm seemingly reasonable estimates that this little book has, since its appearance in 1783, sold something approaching 100 million copies. Marketed in the "modern" method of paperback books, side by side with the salt and the calico of the general store, Webster's speller was selling approximately 1 million copies a year at a time when the entire population of the country was less than 10 million. Its consequent influence upon the standard of American spelling is great beyond measurement.

Throughout his own long lifetime, Webster was assiduous in promoting his own system of spelling. He would often give his book free to printers or hand the compositor a printed slip, saying as he did so, "My lad, when you use these words, oblige me by spelling them as here."[1] Thus Webster was able to encourage a uniformity of spelling throughout the United States and to induce Americans to use most of those forms that distinguish American from British spelling to this day. (It is somewhat surprising, therefore, to find, as the reader will in the following selec-

[1] Van Wyck Brooks, *The Flowering of New England* (New York: Dutton, 1952), p. 69.

tions, that Webster, or his printer, tolerated so many inconsistencies in his own work.) He chose the ending "-or" over "-our" in words like "honor" and "color"; he changed the "-re" to "-er" in words like "theater" and "center"; he got rid of a great many doubled consonants in words like "traveler" and "wagon"; he established "s" rather than "c" in words like "defense"; and he made current many spellings that are today characteristically American, such as "jail," "plow," "mold," and "ax." In addition, through the influence of his spelling books and his dictionary, Webster was largely responsible for the great popular interest among Americans in spelling and correctness. The spelling bee, which developed from Webster's system of oral spelling drill, was to grow into as much of an American institution as the husking bee, and his alphabet-method of teaching reading was to prevail in American schools well into the twentieth century.

Of equal interest is the less obvious influence of Webster's work upon the tenor and content of American textbooks, and thus upon the cultural outlook of generations of American youth. This initial volume set the pattern for all of Webster's later schoolbooks (see, for example, Selection Four) in substituting for religious instances and illustrations a series of anecdotes related to the life of the emerging American nation. The homely subject matter of Webster's speller quickly superseded the Calvinist content of Thomas Dilworth's *New Guide to the English Tongue,* then the reigning best seller, and set an ample precedent for another famous schoolbook series, the McGuffey Readers. The appeal of the patriotic motive in textbooks was almost immediately evident when, in 1788, Nicholas Pike published a system of arithmetic "more suitable to our Meridian," as "the United States are now an independent Nation."

The introduction to his first published book is a touchstone to the career of Noah Webster. It suggests his bright vision of the future America, independent of the mother country in manners and morals, as well as in politics, and eminently strong in arts and in arms. A letter written just prior to the appearance of his speller states Webster's conviction that "an attention to literature must be the principal bulwark against the encroachments of civil and ecclesiastical tyrants. . . ." The subsequent history of the volume confirmed his belief that "a little fifteen-penny volume . . . may convey much useful knowledge to the remote, obscure recesses of honest poverty," and amply fulfilled his hope that "a person of my youth may have some influence in exciting a spirit of literary industry" in the embryonic nation.[2]

[2] Letter to John Canfield, January 6, 1783, in Warfel, *Letters of Noah Webster,* pp. 3–4.

"*American Glory Begins to Dawn . . .*"

To attack deep rooted prejudices and oppose the current of opinion, is a task of great difficulty and hazard. It commonly requires length of time and favourable circumstances to diffuse and establish a sentiment among the body of the people; but when a sentiment has acquired the stamp of time and the authority of general custom, it is too firm to be shaken by the efforts of an individual. Even errour becomes too sacred to be violated by the assaults of innovation.

But the present period is an aera of wonders. Greater changes have been wrought in the minds of men in the short compass of eight years past than are commonly effected in a century.

Previously to the late war, America preserved the most unshaken attachment to Great Britain. The king, the constitution, the laws, the commerce, the fashions, the books, and even the sentiments of Englishmen were implicitly supposed to be the *best* on earth. Not only their virtues and improvements, but their prejudices, their errours, their vices, and their follies were adopted by us with avidity. But by a concurrence of those powerful causes that effect almost instantaneous revolutions in states, the political views of America have suffered a total change. She now sees a mixture of profound wisdom and consummate folly in the British constitution; a ridiculous compound of freedom and tyranny in their laws; and a few struggles of patriotism, overpowered by the corruptions of a wicked administration. She views the vices of that nation with abhorrence, their errours with pity, and their follies with contempt.

While the Americans stand astonished at their former delusion and enjoy the pleasure of a final separation from their insolent sovereigns, it becomes their duty to attend to the *arts of peace*, and particularly to the interests of literature, to see if there be not some errours to be corrected, some defects to be supplied, and some improvements to be introduced into our systems of education, as well as into those of civil policy. We find Englishmen practising upon very erroneous maxims in politics and religion; and possibly we shall find, upon careful examination, that their methods of education are equally erroneous and defective.

The British writers remark it as one of the follies of their nation that they have attended more to the study of ancient and foreign languages than to the improvement of their own. The ancient Greek and Roman languages, and the modern French and Italian, have generally been made a necessary part of a polite or learned education, while a grammatical study of their own language has, till very lately, been totally neglected. This ridiculous practice has found its way to America, and so violent have been the prejudices in support of it that the whispers of common sense in favour of our native tongue have been silenced amidst the clamour of pedantry in favour of Greek and Latin.

The consequence is that few attempts have been made to reduce our language to rules and expunge the corruptions that ignorance and caprice, unguided by any standard, must necessarily introduce. It is but a short time since we have had a grammar of our own tongue, formed upon the true principles of its Saxon original. And those who have given us the most perfect systems have confined themselves chiefly to the two last branches of grammar, Analogy and Syntax. In the two first, Orthography and Prosody—that is, in the spelling and pronunciation of words—we have no guide, or none but such as lead into innumerable errours. The want of some standard in schools has occasioned a great variety of dialects in Great Britain and, of course, in America. Every county in England, every state in America, and almost every town in each state has some peculiarities in pronunciation which are equally erroneous and disagreeable to its neighbours. And how can these distinctions be avoided? The sounds of our letters are more capricious and irregular than those of any alphabet with which we are acquainted. Several of our vowels have four or five different sounds, and the same sounds are often expressed by five, six, or seven different characters. The case is much the same with our consonants. And these different sounds have no mark of distinction. How would a child or a foreigner learn the different sounds of *o* in these words, *rove, move, dove,* or of *oo* in *poor, door?* Or that *a, ai, ei,* and *e* have precisely the same sound in these words, *bare, laid, vein, there?* Yet these and fifty other irregularities have passed unnoticed by authors of spelling books and dictionaries. They study the language enough to find the difficulties of it—they tell us that it is impossible to reduce it to order—that it is to be learnt only by the ear—they lament the disorder and dismiss it without a remedy.

Thus the pronunciation of our language, tho' the most important and difficult part of grammar, is *left* to parents and nurses, to ignorance and caprice, to custom, accident, or nothing—nay, to something worse, to coxcombs, who have a large share in directing the *polite taste* of pronunciation, which of course is as vicious as that of any other class of people. And while this is the case, every person will claim a right to pronounce most agreably to his own fancy, and the language will be exposed to perpetual fluctuation.

This consideration gave rise to the following little system, which is designed to introduce uniformity and accuracy of pronunciation into common schools. It cost me much labour to form a plan that should be both *simple* and *accurate.* The one here adopted seems to unite these two articles, at least so far as to prevent any material errours. A more accurate method might have been invented, but it must have been too complicated to be useful. The rules for ascertaining a just pronunciation are so simple and concise that I flatter myself they fall within the comprehension of the most indifferent capacity. Some may possibly be too indolent to study them, and others, from a principle of self-sufficiency, may affect to despise them. The former will be modest enough neither to approve nor condemn what they deem beneath their attention; and I would inform the latter that after I had devoted nine years to the acquisition of knowledge, three or four of which were spent in studying languages and about the same period in teaching the English, I was astonished to find myself a stranger to its principal beauties and most obvious faults. Those, therefore, who disdain this attempt to improve our language and assist the instructors of youth must be either much more or much less acquainted with the language than I am. The criticisms of those who know more will be received with gratitude; the censure or ridicule of those who know less will be inexcusable.

The principal part of instructors are illiterate people and require some easy guide to the *standard* of pronunciation, which is nothing else but the customary pronunciation of the most accurate scholars and literary gentlemen. Such a standard, universally used in schools, would, in time, demolish those odious distinctions of provincial dialects which are the objects of reciprocal ridicule in the United States. Not to mention small differences, I would observe that the inhabitants of New England and Virginia have a peculiar pronunciation which affords much diversion to their neighbours. On the other hand, the language in the middle states is tinctured with a variety of Irish, Scotch, and German dialects which are justly censured as deviations from propriety and the standard of elegant pronunciation. The truth is, *usus est Norma Loquendi*— general custom is the rule of speaking—and every deviation from this must be wrong. The dialect of one state is as ridiculous as that of another; each is authorised by local custom, and neither is supported by any superior excellence. If in New England we hear a flat drawling pronunciation, in the more southern states we hear the words *veal, very, vulgar* pronounced *weal, wery, wulgar; wine, winter,* &c., changed into *vine, vinter; soft* becomes *saft;* and *raisins* and *wound,* contrary to all rule and propriety, are pronounced *reesins,* and *woond.* It is the present mode at the southward to pronounce *u* like *yu,* as *virtyue, fortyune,* &c., and in a rapid pronunciation these become *virchue, forchune,* as also *duty, duel,* are changed into *juty, juel.* The advocate for this pronunciation pretend that this is the English sound of *u,* but this can not be true because they do not give *u* the sound of *yu* to one word originally English. It seems to arise rather from an imitation of the French, which has been a remarkable folly of the English nation; or perhaps it originated in a fondness for singularity, which has corrupted the language more than all the ignorance of the vulgar. But every innovation of this kind ought to be discountenanced.

It would be much more for the reputation of Americans to unite in destroying provincial and local distinctions, in resisting the stream of corruptions that is ever flowing from ignorance and pride, and in establishing one uniform standard of elegant pronunciation, than to blend two different languages together by applying French sounds to English words, to suffer the structure of our language to be constantly changing and its beauty to be disfigured by every coxcomb.[3]

*   *   *

The author's intention is certainly good—he wishes to render the acquisition of our language easy and the pronunciation accurate and uniform. The necessity of reforming our present method of instruction was suggested by his own experience, and the plan here adopted has been pursued with increasing conviction that, if well executed, it would be extensively useful. He feels diffident of his own abilities in this arduous and delicate undertaking, but is induced, by the opinion of better judges, to hazard an edition and submit the performance to public scrutiny. Whatever innovations are admitted into the work are warranted by reason, experience, or the authority of eminent scholars. On these the author rests the work and hopes for a favourable reception. Mankind are always startled at *new things;* they believe a thing *right* and *best* because they have never suspected otherwise or because it is the general opinion. But *custom* or the *run of opinion* is only presumptive evidence that a thing is *right* and no proof at all that it is *best.* A person of *sense* must have *better* evidence before he believes either.

---

[3] Webster's outline of the contents of his *A Grammatical Institute of the English Language* and his criticism of Dilworth's *New Guide to the English Tongue* have been omitted. Also omitted is Webster's explanation of the absence of any reference to the Deity. "Frequent thoughtless repetition of that sacred word," he says, leads children to use it with "indifference." "Let *sacred* things be appropriated to *sacred purposes.*"—Ed.

Those who rail so much at *new things* ought to consider that every improvement in life was once *new*—the reformation by Luther was once *new*, the Christian religion was once *new*—nay, their favourite Dilworth was once a *new thing*. And had *these* and other *new things* never been introduced, we should have all, this moment, been pagans and savages.

The author feels the danger to which he exposes himself by this publication. He foresees that some will find fault with it because they think it has merit, others because they think it has none. Some will condemn it from motives of prejudice, some from ignorance, some perhaps from worse motives, and not a few, who seldom look further than the title page, will gravely enquire, with the harmless Israelite of old, *whether any good thing can come out of Nazareth?*

So much may be relied on, that whoever studies the language with half the attention the author has will be convinced there is room enough for amendments in every part of grammar.

Books of this kind have generally been ushered into the world under the patronage of great names. The author sincerely laments the necessity of this practice, and is determined to adopt it only in part. The favourable sentiments of a few gentlemen of eminence, offered to the public in another channel, will be sufficient to excite their attention to the performance. Then if it have merit, it will make its own way in the world; if it have not, the author chuses not, by any means, to use the authority of respectable names to impose a worthless production upon his countrymen. He chuses rather to see it buried in universal neglect. The plan has the approbation of some principal literary characters, not only in Connecticut but in the states of New York, New Jersey, and Pennsylvania.

The author wishes to promote the honour and prosperity of the confederated republics of America and chearfully throws his mite into the common treasure of patriotic exertions. This country must in some future time be as distinguished by the superiority of her literary improvements as she is already by the liberality of her civil and ecclesiastical constitutions. Europe is grown old in folly, corruption, and tyranny—in that country laws are perverted, manners are licentious, literature is declining, and human nature debased. For America in her infancy to adopt the present maxims of the old world would be to stamp the wrinkles of decrepid age upon the bloom of youth and to plant the seeds of decay in a vigourous constitution. American glory begins to dawn at a favourable period and under flattering circumstances. We have the experience of the whole world before our eyes; but to receive indiscriminately the maxims of government, the manners, and the literary taste of Europe and make them the ground on which to build our systems in America must soon convince us that a durable and stately edifice can never be erected upon the mouldering pillars of antiquity. It is the business of *Americans* to select the wisdom of all nations as the basis of her constitutions, to avoid their errours, to prevent the introduction of foreign vices and corruptions and check the career of her own, to promote virtue and patriotism, to embellish and improve the sciences, to diffuse an uniformity and purity of *language,* to add superiour dignity to this infant empire and to human nature.

"... Improving the Advantages and Perpetuating the Union ..."

From *Sketches of American Policy*, Part IV, 1785

EDITOR'S COMMENTS

By 1785, seven years out of Yale and twenty-seven years of age, Noah Webster had tried his hand at schoolteaching, law, and writing schoolbooks, but was without plans for a career. Lacking these and any family ties, yet possessed of a keen desire to play an influential role in the affairs of his country, Webster ventured, in the turmoil of the Confederation, a bold step into national affairs. It may be marked as characteristic of the times, as well as evidence of Webster's self-assurance, that one of so little apparent qualifications would undertake to publish *Sketches of American Policy*, an ambitious treatise on the theory and practice of political science. Webster himself in later years regarded most of the volume as "chimerical," though he never repudiated the fourth sketch, from which the accompanying selection is taken.

Webster took copies of his *Sketches of American Policy* with him on a lecture tour shortly after its publication and distributed them widely among influential acquaintances. The tour, designed to promote the sale of his *A Grammatical Institute of the English Language* and to protect his interests in it through the adoption of adequate copyright legislation, took Webster to major cities from South Carolina to New Hampshire between May, 1785, and November, 1786. The presentation to General Washington of a copy of his *Sketches*—subsequently read by James Madison—lent substance to Webster's later belief that he had been instrumental in bringing about the Constitutional Convention and the document to which it gave birth. Quite apart from the validity of this opinion, Webster's efforts in behalf of a more vigorous national government through the medium of the *Sketches*, his earlier anonymous letters in the Connecticut *Courant*, and his later advocacy of the proposed Constitution support his claim that he knew of "no other person who took the same active part or who devoted half the time to the subject" of political union.[1]

The fourth of Webster's *Sketches*, entitled "Plan of Policy for Improving the Advantages and Perpetuating the Union of the American States," argued that the disappearance of the wartime threat to common safety had revealed serious weaknesses in the Articles of Confederation, which, in turn, led to political disunity and commercial chaos, as evidenced in Shays's Rebellion and in Rhode Island's solitary refusal to approve a national impost. The sketch is a plea for the voluntary surrender of a degree of state sovereignty to a stronger Congress, analogous in its authority over national concerns to the authority of state legislatures within the boundaries of their own states. Although lacking detailed proposals, it is nonetheless an effective appeal for the kind of central government adopted soon afterward. It is also, in its closing paragraphs, a strong plea for cultural, as well as political, unity—the promotion of education, industry, and independence in manners and fashion, since *"all* are essential to our peace and prosperity."

[1] Letter to James Kent, October 20, 1804, in Warfel, *Letters of Noah Webster*, pp. 257–60. See also the facsimile edition of *Sketches of American Policy*.

"...*Improving the Advantages and Perpetuating the Union*..."

I have already mentioned three principles which have generally operated in combining the members of society under some supreme power: a standing army, religion, and fear of an external force. A standing army is necessary in all despotic governments. Religion, by which I mean superstition or human systems of absurdity, is an engine used in almost all governments and has a powerful effect where people are kept in ignorance. The fear of conquest is an infallible bond of union where states are surrounded by martial enemies. After people have been long accustomed to obey, whatever be the first motive of their obedience, there is formed a habit of subordination, which has an almost irresistible influence and which will preserve the tranquillity of government even when coercion or the first principle of obedience has ceased to operate.

None of the foregoing principles can be the bond of union among the American states. A standing army will probably never exist in America. It is the instrument of tyranny and ought to be forever banished from free governments. Religion will have little or no influence in preserving the union of the states. The Christian religion is calculated to cherish a spirit of peace and harmony in society, but will not balance the influence of jarring interests in different governments. As to neighbouring foes, we have none to fear, and European nations are too wise or have too much business at home to think of conquering these states.

We must therefore search for new principles in modelling our political system. The American constitutions are founded on principles different from those of all nations, and we must find new bonds of union to perpetuate the confederation.

In the first place, there must be a supreme power at the head of the union, vested with authority to make laws that respect the states in general and to compel obedience to those laws. Such a power must exist in every society or no man is safe.

In order to understand the nature of such a power, we must recur to the principles explained under the first head of these observations.

All power is vested in the people. That this is their natural and unalienable right is a position that will not be disputed. The only question is how this power shall be exerted to effect the ends of government. If the people retain the power of executing laws, we have seen how this division will destroy all its effect. Let us apply the definition of a perfect system of government to the American states: *The right of making laws for the United States should be vested in all their inhabitants by legal and equal representation, and the right of executing those laws committed to the smallest possible number of magistrates, chosen annually by Congress and responsible to them for their administration.* Such a system of continental government is perfect—it is practicable—and may be rendered permanent. I will venture to assert that such a system may have, in legislation, all the security of republican circumspection and, in administration, all the energy and decision of a monarchy.

But must the powers of Congress be increased? This question implies gross ignorance of the nature of government. The question ought to be, must the American states be united? And if this question is decided in the affirmative, the next question is whether the states can be said to be united without a legislative head? Or, in other words, whether thirteen states can be said to be united in government when each state reserves to itself the sole powers of legislation? The answer to all such questions is extremely easy. If the states propose to form and preserve a confederacy, there must be a supreme head in which the power of all the states is united.

There must be a supreme head, clothed with the same power to make and enforce laws respecting the general policy of all the states as the legislatures of the respective states have to make laws binding on those states respecting their own internal policy. The truth of this is taught by the principles of government and confirmed by the experience of America. Without such a head, the states cannot be *united,* and all attempts to conduct the measures of the continent will prove but governmental farces. So long as any individual state has power to defeat the measures of the other twelve, our pretended union is but a name, and our confederation a cobweb.

What, it will be asked, must the states relinquish their sovereignty and independence, and give Congress their rights of legislation? I beg to know what we mean by *United States?* If after Congress have passed a resolution of a general tenor the states are still at liberty to comply or refuse, I must insist that they are not *united;* they are as *seperate* as they ever were, and Congress is merely an advisory body. If people imagine that Congress ought to be merely a council of advice, they will some time or other discover their most egregious mistake. If three millions of people, united under thirteen different heads, are to be governed or brought to act in concert by a *Resolve, That it be recommended,* I confess myself a stranger to history and to human nature.[2] The very idea of uniting discordant interests and restraining the selfish and the wicked principles of men by advisory resolutions is too absurd to have advocates even among illiterate peasants. The resolves of Congress are always treated with respect, and during the late war they were efficacious. But their efficacy proceeded from a principle of common safety which united the interests of all the states; but peace has removed that principle, and the states comply with or refuse the requisitions of Congress just as they please.

The idea of each state preserving its sovereignty and independence in their full latitude, and yet holding up the appearance of a confederacy and a concert of measures, is a solecism in politics that will sooner or later dissolve the pretended union or work other

---

[2] If the states cannot be brought to act in concert now, how can it be done when the number of the states is augmented and the inhabitants multiplied to many millions?

mischiefs sufficient to bear conviction to every mind.

But what shall be done? What system of government shall be framed to guard our rights, to cement our union, and give energy to public measures? The answers to these questions are obvious and a plan of confederacy extremely easy. Let the government of the United States be formed upon the general plan of government in each of the several states.[3]

*   *   *

Let a similar system of government [to that of Connecticut] be extended to the United States. As towns and cities are as to their small matters, sovereign and independent, and as to their general concerns, mere subjects of the state, so let the several states, as to their own policy, be sovereign and independent, but as to the common concerns of all, let them be mere subjects of the federal head. If the necessity of a union is admitted, such a system is the only means of effecting it. However independent each state may be and ought to be in things that relate to itself merely, yet as a part of a greater body it must be a subject of that body in matters that relate to the whole.

A system of continental government thus organized may establish and perpetuate the confederation without infringing the rights of any particular state.[4] But the power of all the states must be reduced to a narrow compass—it must center in a single body of men—and it must not be liable to be controlled or defeated by an individual state. The states assembled in Congress must have the same compulsory power in matters that concern the whole as a man has in his own family, as a city has within the limits of the corporation, and as the legislature of a state has in the limits of that state respecting matters that fall within their several jurisdictions.

I beg to know how otherwise the states will be governed as a collective body? Every man knows by his own experience that even families are not to be kept in subordination by recommendations and advice. How much less then will such flimsy things command

[3] Webster's description of Connecticut's government has been omitted.—Ed.
[4] Webster's footnote, drawing a celestial analogy, has been omitted.—Ed.

the obedience of a whole continent? They will not—they do not. A single state [Rhode Island], by non-compliance with resolves of Congress, has repeatedly defeated the most salutary measures of the states proposed by Congress and acceded to by twelve out of thirteen.[5]

I will suppose for the present that a measure recommended by Congress and adopted by a majority of the legislatures should be really repugnant to the interest of a single state, considered in its seperate capacity. Would it be right for that state to oppose it? While the measure is in agitation it is the undoubted privilege of every state to oppose it by every argument. But when it is passed by the concurrence of a legal majority, it is the duty of every state to acquiesce. So far from resisting the measure, those very individuals who opposed it in debate ought to support it in execution.[6] The reason is very plain—society and government can be supported on no other principles. The interest of individuals must always give place to the interest of the whole community. This principle of government is not perfect, but it is as perfect as any principle that can be carried into effect on this side heaven.

It is for the interest of the American states either to be united or not. If their union is unnecessary, let Congress be annihilated or let them be denominated a *council of advice* and considered as such. They must then be stripped of their power of making peace and war, and of a variety of prerogatives given them by the Articles of Confederation. In this case we ourselves and the states of Europe should know what kind of a being Congress is—what dependence can be placed on their resolves—what is the nature of the treaties which they have made and the debts they have contracted.

But if the states are all serious in a design to establish a permanent *union*, let their sincerity be evinced by their public conduct.

Suppose the legislature of Rhode Island had no power to compel obedience to its laws, but any town in that state had power to defeat every public measure. Could any laws be rendered effectual? Could

---

[5] Webster's illustrative footnote has been omitted.—Ed.
[6] Webster's illustrative footnote has been omitted.—Ed.

it with propriety be called a state? Could it be said that there was any supreme power, or any government? Certainly not. Suppose the small town in Connecticut had power to defeat the most salutary measures of the state. Would not every other town rise in arms against any attempt to exert such a power? They certainly would. The truth of the case is, where the power of a people is not united in some individual or small body of individuals, but continues divided among the members of a society, that power is nothing at all. This fact is clearly proved under the first head of these observations, and more clearly felt by our fatal experience.

The American states, as to their general internal policy, are *not united;* there is no supreme power at their head; they are in a perfect state of nature and independence as to each other; each is at liberty to fight its neighbour, and there is no sovereign to call forth the power of the continent to quell the dispute or punish the agressor.[7] It is not in the power of the Congress—they have no command over the militia of the states—each state commands its own, and should any one be disposed for civil war, the sword must settle the contest and the weakest be sacrificed to the strongest.

It is now in the power of the states to form a continental government as efficacious as the interior government of any particular state.

The general concerns of the continent may be reduced to a few heads, but in all the affairs that respect the whole, Congress must have the same power to enact laws and compel obedience throughout the continent as the legislatures of the several states have in their respective jurisdictions. If Congress have any power, they must have the whole power of the continent. Such a power would not abridge the sovereignty of each state in any article relating to its own government. The internal policy of each state would be still under the sole superintendence of its legislature. But in a matter that equally respects all the states, no individual state has more than a thirteenth part of the legislative authority, and consequently has no right to decide what measure shall or shall not take place on

---

[7] Webster's illustrative footnote has been omitted.—Ed.

the continent. A majority of the states *must* decide;[8] our confederation cannot be permanent unless founded on that principle; nay, more, the states cannot be said to be *united* till such a principle is adopted in its utmost latitude. If a single town or precinct could counteract the will of a whole state, would there be any government in that state? It is an established principle in government that the will of the minority must submit to that of the majority; and a single state, or a minority of states, ought to be disabled to resist the will of the majority as much as a town or county in any state is disabled to prevent the execution of a statute law of the legislature.

It is on this principle and *this alone* that a free state can be governed; it is on this principle alone that the American states can exist as a confederacy of republics. Either the several states must continue seperate, totally independent of each other and liable to all the evils of jealousy, dispute, and civil dissention—nay, liable to a civil war upon any clashing of interests—or they must constitute a general head, composed of representatives from all the states and vested with the power of the whole continent to enforce their decisions. There is no other alternative. One of these events must inevitably take place, and the revolution of a few years will verify the prediction.

I know the objections that have been urged by the supporters of faction, and perhaps by some honest men, against such a power at the head of the states. But the objections all arise from false notions of government or from a wilful design to embroil the states. Many people, I doubt not, really suppose that such power in Congress would be dangerous to the liberties of the states. Such ought to be enlightened.

There are two fundamental errors, very common in the reasonings which I have heard on the powers of Congress. The first arises from the idea that our American constitutions are founded on principles similar to those of the European governments which have been called *free*. Hence people are led into a second error,

---

[8] Congress have been more careful of our liberties; for the Articles of Confederation ordain that, in matters of great national concern, the concurrence, not of *seven* states, a mere majority, but of *nine*, should be requisite to pass a resolution.

which is that Congress are a body independent of their constituents and under the influence of a distinct interest.

But we have seen before that our systems of civil government are different from all others, founded on different principles, more favourable to freedom and more secure against corruption.

We have no perpetual distinctions of property which might raise one class of men above another and create powerful family connections and combinations against our liberties. We suffer no hereditary offices or titles which might breed insolence and pride and give their possessors an opportunity to oppress their fellow men. We are not under the direction of a bigoted clergy who might rob us of the means of knowledge and then inculcate on credulous minds what sentiments they please. Not a single office or emolument in America is held by prescription or hereditary right, but all at the disposal of the people; and not a man on the continent, but drones and villains, who has not the privilege of frequently choosing his legislators and impeaching his magistrates for mal-administration. Such principles form the basis of our American governments, the first and only governments on earth that are founded on the true principles of equal liberty and properly guarded from corruption.

The legislatures of the American states are the only legislatures on earth which are *wholly* dependent on the people at large, and Congress is as dependent on the several states as the legislatures are on their constituents. The members of Congress are chosen by the legislatures,[9] removable by them at pleasure, dependent on them for subsistence, and responsible to their constituents for their conduct. But this is not all. After having been delegated three years, the confederation renders them ineligible for the term of three years more, when they must return, mingle with the people, and become private citizens. At the same time, their interest is the same with that of the people; for, enjoying no exclusive privileges but what are temporary, they cannot knowingly enact oppressive

---

[9] In eleven states. In the other two, they are elected by the people. This is a defect, however, in the constitutions of those states, as the delegates, when chosen by the people, are immediately removable by the assembly and their place may be supplied without a reason given. The privilege of the people therefore is nothing.

laws, because they involve themselves, their families, and estates in all the mischiefs that result from such laws.

People, therefore, who attempt to terrify us with apprehensions of losing our liberties because other states have lost theirs betray an ignorance of history and of the principles of our confederation. I will not undertake to say that the government of the American states will not be corrupted or degenerate into tyranny. But I venture to assert that if it should, it will be the fault of the people. If the people continue to choose their representatives annually and the choice of delegates to Congress should remain upon its present footing, that body can never become tyrants. A measure partially oppressive may be resolved upon, but while the principles of representation, which are always in the power of the people, remain uncorrupted, such a measure can be of no long continuance. The best constitution of government may degenerate from its purity through a variety of causes, but the confederation of these states is better secured than any government on earth and less liable to corruption from any quarter.

There is the same danger that the constitutions of the several states will become tyrannical as that the principles of federal government will be corrupted. The states in their collective capacity have no more reason to dread an uncontrolable power in Congress than they have, in their individual capacity, to dread the uncontrolable power of their own legislatures. Their security in both instances is an equal representation, the dependence, the responsibility, and the rotation of their representatives. These articles constitute the basis of our liberties and will be an effectual security so long as the people are wise enough to maintain the principles of the confederation.[10]

*   *   *

What do the states obtain by reserving to themselves the right of deciding on the propriety of the resolutions of Congress? The great advantage of having every measure defeated, our frontiers

---

[10] A paragraph on the value of fixed constitutions in resisting tyranny has been omitted.—Ed.

exposed to savages, the debts of the states unpaid and accumulating, national faith violated, commerce restricted and insulted, one state filching some interest from another, and the whole body, linked together by cobwebs and shadows, the jest and the ridicule of the world. This is not a chimerical description; it is a literal representation of facts as they now exist. One state found it could make some advantage by refusing the impost. Congress have reasoned with their legislature and by incontrovertible proofs have pointed out the impropriety of the refusal, but all to no purpose. Thus one fiftieth part of the states counteracts a measure that the other states suppose not only beneficial but necessary, a measure on which the discharge of our public debt and our national faith most obviously depend. Can a government thus feeble and disjointed answer any valuable purpose? Can commutative justice between the states ever be obtained? Can public debts be discharged and credit supported? Can America ever be respected by her enemies when one of her own states can, year after year, abuse her weakness with impunity? No; the American states, so celebrated for their wisdom and valour in the late struggle for freedom and empire, will be the contempt of nations unless they can unite their force and carry into effect all the constitutional measures of Congress, whether those measures respect themselves or foreign nations.

The Articles of Confederation ordain that the public expenses shall be defayed out of a common treasury. But where is this treasury? Congress prescribe a measure for supplying this treasury, but the states do not approve of the measure; each state will take its own way and its own time, and perhaps not supply its contingent of money at all. Is this an adherence to the articles of our union? It certainly is not, and the states that refuse a compliance with the general measures of the continent would, under a good government, be considered as rebels. Such a conduct amounts to treason, for it strikes at the foundation of government.

Permit me to ask every candid American how society could exist if every man assumed the right of sacrificing his neighbour's property to his own interest? Are there no rights to be relinquished, no sacrifices to be made for the sake of enjoying the

benefits of civil government? If every town in Rhode Island, even
the smallest, could annihilate every act of the legislature, could
that state exist? Were such a selfish system to prevail generally,
there would be an end of government, and civil society would
become a curse. A social state would be less eligible than a savage
state in proportion as knowledge would be increased and knaves
multiplied. Local inconveniences and local interests never ought to
disappoint a measure of general utility. If there is not power
enough in government to remedy these evils by obliging private
interests to give way to public, discord will pervade the state and
terminate in a revolution. Such a power must exist somewhere, and
if people will quarrel with good government, there are innumerable opportunities for some daring ambitious genius to erect a
monarchy on civil dissensions. In America there is no danger of an
aristocracy, but the transition from popular anarchy to monarchy is
very natural and often very easy. If these states have any change of
government to fear, it is a monarchy. Nothing but the creation of a
sovereign power over the whole, with authority to compel obedience to legal measures, can ever prevent a revolution in favour of
one monarchy or more. This event may be distant, but is not the
less certain. America has it now in her power to create a supreme
power over the whole continent, sufficient to answer all the ends of
government without abridging the rights or destroying the sovereignty of a single state. But should the extreme jealousy of the
states prevent the lodgment of such a power in a body of men
chosen by themselves and removable at pleasure, such a power will
inevitably create itself in the course of events.

The confederation has sketched out a most excellent form of
continental government. The ninth article recites the powers of
Congress, which are perhaps nearly sufficient to answer the ends of
our union, were there any method of enforcing their resolutions. It
is there said what powers shall be exercised by Congress, but no
penalty is annexed to disobedience. What purpose would the laws
of a state answer if they might be evaded with impunity and if
there were no penalty annexed to a breach of them? A law without
a penalty is mere *advice;* a magistrate without the power of
punishing is a *cypher.* Here is the *great defect* in the articles of our

federal government. Unless Congress can be vested with the same authority to compel obedience to their resolutions that a legislature in any state has to enforce obedience to the laws of that state, the existence of such a body is entirely needless and will not be of long duration. I repeat what I have before said. The idea of governing thirteen states and uniting their interest by mere *resolves* and *recommendations,* without any penalty annexed to a non-compliance, is a ridiculous farce, a burlesque on government, and a reproach to America.

Let Congress be empowered to call forth the force of the continent, if necessary, to carry into effect those measures which they have a right to frame. Let the president be, *ex officio,* supreme magistrate, cloathed with authority to execute the laws of Congress in the same manner as the governors of the states are to execute the laws of the states. Let the superintendent of finance have the power of receiving the public monies and issuing warrants for collection in the manner the treasurer has in Connecticut. Let every executive officer have power to enforce the laws which fall within his province. At the same time, let them be accountable for their administration. Let penalties be annexed to every species of maladministration and exacted with such rigour as is due to justice and the public safety. In short, let the whole system of legislation be the peculiar right of the delegates in Congress, who are always under the control of the people; and let the whole administration be vested in magistrates as few as possible in number and subject to the control of Congress only. Let every precaution be used in *framing* laws, but let no part of the subjects be able to resist the execution. Let the people keep, and *forever keep,* the sole right of legislation in their own representatives, but divest themselves wholly of any right of directing its own internal affairs, but give to Congress the sole right of conducting the general affairs of the continent. Such a plan of government is practicable and, I believe, the only plan that will preserve the faith, the dignity, and the union of these American states.

I shall just hint several other matters that may serve, in a more remote manner, to confirm the union of these states.

Education or a general diffusion of knowledge among all classes

of men is an article that deserves peculiar attention. Science liberal-
izes men and removes the most inveterate prejudices. Every prejudice, every dissocial passion is an enemy to a friendly intercourse
and the fuel of discord. Nothing can be more illiberal than the
prejudices of the Southern states against New England manners.
They deride our manners and by that derision betray the want of
manners themselves. However different may be the customs and
fashions of different states, yet those of the Southern are as
ridiculous as those of the Northern. The fact is, neither one nor the
other are the subjects of ridicule and contempt. Particular districts
have local peculiarities, but custom gives all an equal degree of
propriety. It is remarked of the Greeks as a great indelicacy of
manners that they held all the world, except themselves, to be
barbarians. The people of Congo think the world to be the work of
angels, except their own country, which they hold to be the work
of the supreme architect. The Greenlanders make a mock of
Europeans, or Kablunets, as they call them. They despise arts and
sciences and value themselves on their skill in catching seals, which
they conceive to be the only useful art.[11] Just as absurd as these are
the prejudices between the states. Education will gradually eradi-
cate them, and a growing intercourse will harmonize the feelings
and the views of all the citizens.

Next to the removal of local prejudices, the annihilation of local
interests between the states deserves their consideration. Each state
wishes to enrich itself as much a possible, but it never ought to be
done at the expence of a neighbour. All imposts and duties upon
goods purchased of one state by another or carried in a port of
another state, either by necessity or accident, are the effect of
narrow views and of selfish, unsociable, ungenerous principles that
degrade any state where they operate. The states may lay what
duties they please upon foreigners—this is no more than honest—
but they ought to consider their several interests as one; they
ought to encourage the commerce of each other; they ought to
promote such an intercourse as will conciliate rather than alienate

---

[11] Webster's footnote containing reflections on Southern taste has been omitted.
—Ed.

each other's affections. Every injury done by any particular state to the union will ultimately recoil upon itself with accumulated weight. It is the act of a madman to sacrifice the happiness of his life to a moment's pleasure, and none but a fool would pull the house about his ears to find a shilling. So long as the states are making every advantage out of each other, racking invention to enlarge their own bounds and augment their wealth and respectability at each other's expence, jealousy, ill-will, and reproaches will disturb the harmony of public measures and contribute to the dissolution of all continental connections. Not only should the states avoid wringing property from each other by duties on articles of commerce, but also an extention of territory in such a manner as to create reciprocal jealousies. All the superior respectability that a single state gains above others by its extent and wealth detracts so much from the strength and harmony of the union. In order to have our union complete and permanent, all the states should have an equal influence in public deliberations. The want of such equality is a capital misfortune; it had well nigh prevented our confederation and has produced other sensible inconveniences.[12]

* * *

America is an independent empire, and ought to assume a national character. Nothing can be more ridiculous than a servile imitation of the manners, the language, and the vices of foreigners. For, setting aside the infancy of our government and our inability to support the fashionable amusements of Europe, nothing can betray a more despicable disposition in Americans than to be the apes of Europeans. An American ought not to ask what is the custom of London and Paris, but what is proper for us in our circumstances and what is becoming our dignity. Instead of this, what is the fact? Why, every fashionable folly is brought from Europe and adopted without scruple in our dress, our manners, and our conversation. All our ladies, even those of the most scanty fortune, must dress like a dutchess in London; every shopkeeper

---

[12] Webster's observations on slavery and the rights of clergymen to hold office have been omitted.—Ed.

must be as great a rake as an English lord; while the *belles* and the *beaux,* with tastes too refined for a vulgar language, must, in all their discourse, mingle a spice of *san souce* and *je ne scai quoi.*

But there is no reasoning with custom nor with fashion. We shall probably learn the arts and virtues of Europeans, but certainly their vices and follies. In politics, our weakness will render us the dupes of their power and artifice; in manners, we shall be the slaves of their barbers and their coxcombs.

But, however important may be the remote consequences of a corruption of manners, yet much nearer concerns now demand our attention. Our union is so feeble that no provision is made for discharging our debts. France calls for interest, and that seriously. Our credit, our faith solemnly pledged, is at stake. Unless we constitute a power at the head of the states sufficient to compel them to act in concert, I now predict not only a dissolution of our federal connection, but a rupture with our national creditors. A war in Europe may possibly suspend this event, but it must certainly take place unless we sacrifice our jealousy to our true interest.

Three things demand our early and careful attention: a general diffusion of knowledge; the encouragement of industry, frugality, and virtue; and a sovereign power at the head of the states. *All* are essential to our peace and prosperity, but on an energetic continental government principally depend our tranquility at home and our respectability among foreign nations.

We ought to generalize our ideas and our measures. We ought not to consider ourselves as inhabitants of a particular state only, but as *Americans,* as the common subjects of a great empire. We cannot and ought not wholly to divest ourselves of provincial views and attachments, but we should subordinate them to the general interests of the continent. As a member of a family every individual has some domestic interests; as a member of a corporation he has other interests; as an inhabitant of a state he has a more extensive interest; as a citizen and subject of the American empire he has a national interest far superior to all others. Every relation in society constitutes some obligations, which are proportional to the magnitude of the society. A good prince does not ask what will be for the interest of a county or small district in his dominions, but what will promote the prosperity of his kingdom. In the same manner, the citizens of this new world should enquire not what will aggrandize this town or this state, but what will augment the power, secure the tranquility, multiply the subjects, and advance the opulence, the dignity, and the virtues of the United States. Self-interest, both in morals and politics, is and ought to be the ruling principle of mankind, but this principle must operate in perfect conformity to social and political obligations. Narrow views and illiberal prejudices may for a time produce a selfish system of politics in each state, but a few years' experience will correct our ideas of self-interest and convince us that a selfishness which excludes others from a participation of benefits is, in all cases, self-ruin, and that *provincial interest* is inseperable from *national interest*.

A note written by
Webster on the letter by
Thomas Fitzsimmons
that inspired the writing of
*An Examination into the
Leading Principles of
the Federal Constitution.*

"... Americans Must Cease to Contend ..."

From *An Examination into the Leading Principles of
the Federal Constitution Proposed by the Late
Convention Held at Philadelphia,* 1787

EDITOR'S COMMENTS

Webster was in Philadelphia during the framing of the Constitution, teaching at the Episcopal Academy. His diary reveals that he was frequently in the company of "Convention Gentlemen"—Washington himself paid a call on him during this period—indicating that at twenty-nine he was already winning a place for himself in Federalist circles.

On September 15, 1787, Thomas Fitzsimmons, a delegate to the Convention from Pennsylvania, wrote Webster that his "abilities might be eminently useful" in winning popular support for the new Constitution, at that moment being completed.[1] Eager to play a part in promoting a strong central government, particularly one so closely resembling that proposed in his *Sketches of American Policy*, Webster leaped at the opportunity. In two days he wrote the pamphlet from which the accompanying selection is taken, *An Examination into the Leading Principles of the Federal Constitution Proposed by the Late Convention Held at Philadelphia*.

A point-by-point analysis of the historic document, supplemented by typically Websterian observations on nationalism and government, the essay is the work of an effective eighteenth-century publicist. Webster signed it "A Citizen of America," probably because he already felt, as he wrote Washington in 1790, that essays bearing his name "would not meet with the consideration they might deserve."[2] In it Webster's ability to marshal a variety of arguments, designed to appeal to a wide range of people, in support of his views was clearly demonstrated. The favored themes that the states under the "cobweb" of confederation were in little more than "a state of nature" and that a strong central government

[1] From a letter in the New York Public Library.
[2] Quoted in Warfel, *Letters of Noah Webster*, p. 86.

was necessary for the preservation of liberty dominate the composition; but Webster again makes an energetic case for property ownership as a foundation of liberty, a belief that was soon to be strengthened by his return to the "Steady Habit" Federalist state of Connecticut, where broad distribution of property made the view seem less "aristocratic" than in some parts of the nation. Webster's conviction that civil power rested in property prompted him to argue against a bill of rights in the Constitution, on the ground that a general distribution of property in America was better insurance for civil liberties than any legal or constitutional guarantee.

The handwritten notes on Webster's personal copy of the *Examination* afford an excellent insight into his later political disillusionment. Where in 1787 he had assured his readers that the proposed method for electing the President "excludes the danger of faction and corruption," he later inserted the comment, "This proves how little dependence can be placed on theory. Twelve years' experience, or four elections, demonstrate the contrary." But the accompanying selection shows Webster at his confident, buoyant best, championing the cause of political union, the first and most urgent step toward true independence and lasting liberty.

"... Americans Must Cease to Contend ..."

Of all the memorable aeras that have marked the progress of men from the savage state to the refinements of luxury, that which has combined them into society under a wise system of government and given form to a nation has ever been recorded and celebrated as the most important. Legislators have ever been deemed the greatest benefactors of mankind—respected when living, and often deified after their death. Hence the fame of Fohi [Fu Hsi] and Confucius, Moses, Solon, and Lycurgus of Romulus and Numa, of Alfred, Peter the Great, and Mango Capac [founder of the Inca Dynasty], whose names will be celebrated through all ages for framing and improving constitutions of government which introduced order into society and secured the benefits of law to millions of the human race.

This western world now beholds an aera important beyond conception, and which posterity will number with the age of Czar of Muscovy and with the promulgation of the Jewish laws at Mount Sinai. The names of those men who have digested a system of constitutions for the American empire will be enrolled with those of Zamolxis [Zalmoxis] and Odin, and celebrated by posterity with the honors which less enlightened nations have paid to the fabled demi-gods of antiquity.

But the origin of the AMERICAN REPUBLIC is distinguished by peculiar circumstances. Other nations have been driven together by fear and necessity—their governments have generally been the result of a single man's observations or the offspring of particular interests. In the formation of our constitution the wisdom of all ages is collected—the legislators of antiquity are consulted, as well as the opinions and interests of the millions who are concerned. In short, it is an *empire of reason.*

In the formation of such a government it is not only the *right,* but the indispensable *duty,* of every citizen to examine the principles of it, to compare them with the principles of other governments with a constant eye to our particular situation and circumstances, and thus endeavor to foresee the future operations of our own system and its effects upon human happiness.[3]

*   *   *

But I cannot quit this subject without attempting to correct some erroneous opinions respecting *freedom* and *tyranny* and the principles by which they are supported. Many people seem to entertain an idea that liberty consists in a *power to act without any control.* This is more liberty than even the savages enjoy. But in civil society political liberty consists in *acting conformably to the sense of a majority of the society.* In a free government every man binds himself to obey the *public voice,* or the opinions of a majority, and the *whole society* engages to *protect each individual.* In such a government a man is *free* and safe. But reverse the case; suppose every man to act without control or fear of punishment—every man would be free, but no man would be sure of his freedom one moment. Each would have the power of taking his neighbor's life, liberty, or property, and no man would command more than his own strength to repel the invasion. The case is the same with states. If the states should not unite into one compact society, every state may trespass upon its neighbor, and the injured state has no means of redress but its own military force.

The present situation of our American states is very little better than a state of nature—our boasted state sovereignties are so far from securing our liberty and property that they, every moment, expose us to the loss of both. That state which commands the heaviest purse and longest sword may at any moment lay its

[3] Webster's detailed commentary on the proposed constitution has been omitted. —Ed.

weaker neighbor under tribute, and there is no superior power now existing that can regularly oppose the invasion or redress the injury. From such liberty, O Lord, deliver us!

But what is tyranny? Or how can a free people be deprived of their liberties? Tyranny is the exercise of some power over a man which is not warranted by law or necessary for the public safety. A people can never be deprived of their liberties while they retain in their own hands a power superior to any other power in the state. This position leads me directly to enquire, in what consists the power of a nation or of an order of men?

In some nations legislators have derived much of their power from the influence of religion, or from that implicit belief which an ignorant and superstitious people entertain of the gods and their interposition in every transaction of life. The Roman senate sometimes availed themselves of this engine to carry their decrees and maintain their authority. This was particularly the case under the aristocracy which succeeded the abolition of the monarchy. The augurs and priests were taken wholly from patrician families. They constituted a distinct order of men—had power to negative any law of the people by declaring that it was passed during the taking of the auspices.[4] This influence, derived from the authority of opinion, was less perceptible, but as tyrannical as a military force. The same influence constitutes, at this day, a principal support of several governments on the Eastern continent and perhaps in South America. But in North America, by a singular concurrence of circumstances, the possibility of establishing this influence as a pillar of government is totally precluded.

Another source of power in government is a military force. But this, to be efficient, must be superior to any force that exists among the people or which they can command, for otherwise this force would be annihilated on the first exercise of acts of oppression. Before a standing army can rule, the people must be disarmed, as they are in almost every kingdom in Europe. The supreme power in America cannot enforce unjust laws by the sword, because the whole body of the people are armed and constitute a force superior

[4] Webster's Latin references have been omitted.—Ed.

to any band of regular troops that can be, on any pretence, raised in the United States. A military force at the command of Congress can execute no laws but such as the people perceive to be just and constitutional; for they will possess the *power,* and jealousy will instantly inspire the *inclination,* to resist the execution of a law which appears to them unjust and oppressive. In spite of all the nominal powers vested in Congress by the constitution, were the system once adopted in its fullest latitude, still the actual exercise of them would be frequently interrupted by popular jealousy. I am bold to say that *ten* just and constitutional measures would be resisted where *one* unjust or oppressive law would be enforced. The powers vested in Congress are little more than *nominal;* nay, *real* power cannot be vested in them, nor in any body, but in the *people.* The source of power is in the *people* of this country and cannot for ages, and probably never will, be removed.

In what then does *real* power consist? The answer is short and plain—in *property.* Could we want any proofs of this which are not exhibited in this country, the uniform testimony of history will furnish us with multitudes.[5]

*   *   *

A general and tolerably equal distribution of landed property is the whole basis of national freedom. The system of the great Montesquieu will ever be erroneous till the words *property or lands in fee-simple* are substitued for virtue throughout his *Spirit of Laws.*

Virtue, patriotism, or love of country never was and never will be, till men's natures are changed, a fixed, permanent principle and support of government. But in an agricultural country a general possession of land in fee-simple may be rendered perpetual, and the inequalities introduced by commerce are too fluctuating to endanger government. An equality of property, with a necessity of alienation constantly operating to destroy combinations of powerful families, is the very *soul of a republic.* While this continues, the people will inevitably possess both *power* and *freedom;* when this

[5] Webster's illustrations from Roman and British history have been omitted. —Ed.

is lost, power departs, liberty expires, and a commonwealth will inevitably assume some other form.

The liberty of the press, trial by jury, the Habeas Corpus writ, even Magna Charta itself, although justly deemed the palladia of freedom, are all inferior considerations when compared with a general distribution of real property among every class of people.[6] The power of entailing estates is more dangerous to liberty and republican government than all the constitutions that can be written on paper, or even than a standing army. Let the people have property and they *will* have power—a power that will for ever be exerted to prevent a restriction of the press, an abolition of trial by jury, or the abridgement of any other privilege. The liberties of America, therefore, and her forms of government stand on the broadest basis. Removed from the fears of a foreign invasion and

---

[6] Montesquieu supposed *virtue* to be the principle of a republic. He derived his notions of this form of government from the astonishing firmness, courage, and patriotism which distinguished the republics of Greece and Rome. But this *virtue* consisted in pride, contempt of strangers, and a martial enthusiasm which sometimes displayed itself in defence of their country. These principles are never permanent—they decay with refinement, intercourse with other nations, and increase of wealth. No wonder then that these republics declined, for they were not founded on fixed principles, and hence authors imagine that republics cannot be durable. None of the celebrated writers on government seem to have laid sufficient stress on a general possession of real property in fee-simple. Even the author of the *Political Sketches*, in the *Museum* for the month of September, seems to have passed it over in silence, although he combats Montesquieu's system and, to prove it false, enumerates some of the principles which distinguish our government from others and which he supposes constitute the support of republics.

The English writers on law and government consider Magna Charta, trial by juries, the Habeas Corpus act, and the liberty of the press as the bulwarks of freedom. All this is well. But in no government of consequence in Europe is freedom established on its true and immoveable foundation. The property is too much accumulated, and the accumulations too well guarded, to admit the true *principle of republics*. But few centuries have elapsed since the body of the people were vassals. To such men the smallest extension of popular privileges was deemed an invaluable blessing. Hence the encomiums upon trial by juries and the articles just mentioned. But these people have never been able to mount to the source of *liberty, estates in fee*, or at least but partially; they are yet obliged to drink at the streams. Hence the English jealousy of certain rights which are guaranteed by acts of parliament. But in America, and here alone, we have gone at once to the *fountain of liberty* and raised the people to their true dignity. Let the lands be possessed by the people in fee-simple, let the fountain be kept pure, and the streams will be pure of course. Our jealousy of *trial by jury, the liberty of the press*, &c., is totally groundless. Such rights are inseparably connected with the *power* and *dignity* of the people, which rest on their *property*. They cannot be abridged. All *other* nations have wrested *property* and *freedom* from *barons* and *tyrants; we* begin our empire with full possession of property and all its attending rights.

conquest, they are not exposed to the convulsions that shake other governments, and the principles of freedom are so general and energetic as to exclude the possibility of a new change in our republican constitutions.

But while *property* is considered as the *basis* of the freedom of the American yeomanry, there are other auxiliary supports, among which is the *information of the people.* In no country is education so general, in no country have the body of the people such a knowledge of the rights of men and the principles of government. This knowledge, joined with a keen sense of liberty and a watchful jealousy, will guard our constitutions and awaken the people to an instantaneous resistance of encroachments.

But a principal bulwark of freedom is the right of election. An equal distribution of property is the *foundation* of a republic, but *popular elections* form the great *barrier* which defends it from assault and guards it from the slow and imperceptible approaches of corruption. Americans! Never resign that right. It is not very material whether your representatives are elected for one year or two, but the *right* is the Magna Charta of your governments. For this reason, expunge that clause of the new constitution before mentioned which gives Congress an influence in the election of their own body. The *time, place,* and *manner* of chusing senators or representatives are of little or no consequence to Congress. The number of members and the time of meeting in Congress are fixed, but the *choice* should rest solely with the several states. I repeat it—reject the clause with decency, but with unanimity and firmness.

Excepting that clause, the constitution is good—it guarantees the *fundamental principles* of our several constitutions; it guards our rights; and while it vests extensive powers in Congress, it vests no more than are necessary for our union. Without powers lodged somewhere in a single body—fully competent to lay and collect equal taxes and duties, to adjust controversies between different states, to silence contending interests, to suppress insurrection, to regulate commerce, to treat with foreign nations—our confederation is a cobweb, liable to be blown asunder by every blast of faction that is raised in the remotest corner of the United States.

Every motive that can possibly influence men ever to unite

under civil government now urges the unanimous adoption of the new constitution. But in America we are urged to it by a singular necessity. By the local situation of the several states, *a few* command *all* the advantages of commerce. Those states which have no advantages made equal exertions for independence, loaded themselves with immense debts, and now are utterly unable to discharge them, while their richer neighbors are taxing them for their own benefit merely because they *can*. I can prove to a demonstration that Connecticut, which has the heaviest internal or state debt in proportion to its number of inhabitants of any in the union, cannot discharge its debt on any principles of taxation ever yet practised. Yet the state pays in duties at least 100,000 dollars annually on goods consumed by its own people but imported by New York. This sum, could it be saved to the state by an equal system of revenue, would enable that state gradually to sink its debt.[7]

New Jersey and some other states are in the same situation, except that their debts are not so large in proportion to their wealth and population.

The boundaries of the several states were not drawn with a view to independence, and while this country was subject to Great Britain they produced no commercial or political inconveniences. But the revolution has placed things on a different footing. The advantages of some states and the disadvantages of others are so great—and so materially affect the business and interest of each— that nothing but an equalizing system of revenue that shall reduce the advantages to some equitable proportion can prevent a civil war and save the national debt. Such a system of revenue is the *sine qua non* of public justice and tranquillity.

It is absurd for a man to oppose the adoption of the constitution because *he* thinks some part of it defective or exceptionable. Let every man be at liberty to expunge what *he* judges exceptionable, and not a syllable of the constitution will survive the scrutiny. A painter, after executing a masterly piece, requested every spectator to draw a pencil over the part that did not please him; but, to his surprise, he soon found the *whole piece* defaced. Let every man examine the most perfect building by his *own* taste and, like some

[7] Webster's footnote on Connecticut's debt has been omitted.—Ed.

microscopic critics, condemn the *whole* for small deviations from the rules of architecture, and not a part of the *best* constructed fabric would escape. But let *any* man take a *comprehensive view* of the whole, and he will be pleased with the general beauty and proportions and admire the structure. The same remarks apply to the new constitution. I have no doubt that *every* member of the late convention has exceptions to *some part* of the system proposed. Their constituents have the same, and if *every* objection must be removed before we have a national government, the Lord have mercy on us!

Perfection is not the lot of humanity. Instead of censuring the small faults of the constitution, I am astonished that so many clashing interests have been reconciled, and so many sacrifices made to the *general* interest! The mutual concessions made by the gentlemen of the convention reflect the highest honor on their candor and liberality; at the same time, they prove that their minds were deeply impressed with a conviction that such mutual sacrifices are *essential to our union.* They *must* be made sooner or later by every state, or jealousies, local interests, and prejudices will unsheath the sword and some Caesar or Cromwell will avail himself of our divisions and wade to a throne through streams of blood.

It is not our duty as freeman to receive the opinions of any men, however great and respectable, without an examination. But when we reflect that some of the greatest men in America, with the venerable Franklin and the illustrious Washington at their head, *some* of them the fathers and *saviors* of their country, men who have labored at the helm during a long and violent tempest and guided us to the haven of peace—and *all* of them distinguished for their abilities, their acquaintance with ancient and modern governments, as well as with the temper, the passions, the interests, and the wishes of the Americans—when we reflect on these circumstances, it is impossible to resist impressions of respect, and we are almost impelled to suspect our own judgments when we call in question any part of the system which they have recommended for adoption. Not having the same means of information, we are more liable to mistake the nature and tendency of particular articles of the constitution, or the reasons on which they were admitted.

Great confidence therefore should be reposed in the abilities, the zeal, and integrity of that respectable body. But, after all, if the constitution should, in its future operation, be found defective or inconvenient, two thirds of both houses of Congress or the application of two thirds of the legislatures may open the door for amendments. Such improvements may then be made as experience shall dictate.

Let us then consider the *New Federal Constitution*, as it really is, an *improvement* on the best *constitutions* that the world ever saw. In the house of representatives the people of America have an equal voice and suffrage. The choice of the men is placed in the freemen or electors at large, and the frequency of elections and the responsibility of the members will render them sufficiently dependent on their constituents. The senate will be composed of older men, and while their regular dismission from office once in six years will preserve their dependence on their constituents, the duration of their existence will give firmness to their decisions and temper the factions which must necessarily prevail in the other branch. The president of the United States is elective, and, what is a capital improvement on the best governments, the mode of chusing him excludes the danger of faction and corruption. As the supreme executive, he is invested with power to enforce the laws of the union and give energy to the federal government.

The constitution defines the powers of Congress, and every power not expressly delegated to that body remains in the several state legislatures. The sovereignty and the republican form of government of each state is guaranteed by the constitution, and the bounds of jurisdiction between the federal and respective state governments are marked with precision. In theory, it has all the energy and freedom of the British and Roman governments without their defects. In short, the privileges of freemen are interwoven into the very feelings and habits of the Americans; liberty stands on the immoveable basis of a general distribution of property and diffusion of knowledge, but the Americans must cease to contend, to fear, and to hate before they can realize the benefits of independence and government or enjoy the blessings which heaven has lavished in rich profusion upon this western world.

"... The Revolution ... Was but Just Begun"

From "Remarks on the Manners, Government, Laws, and Domestic Debt of America," in *An American Selection of Lessons in Reading and Speaking*, Part III of *A Grammatical Institute of the English Language*, 1787

EDITOR'S COMMENTS

In many respects the half decade after 1783 marks the zenith of Webster's nationalistic fervor. As yet unsullied by the political involvement of his newspaper career and the disillusion that followed on the heels of the French Revolution and the demise of Washingtonian Federalism, full of the vigor and confidence of youth, and already winning the respect of national leaders, Webster accomplished much during this brief period. His *Sketches of American Policy* (1785) and his *An Examination into the Leading Principles of the Federal Constitution* (1787) fairly bristled with militant sentiment in favor of a strong and independent America. The cultural nationalism of his *The American Spelling Book* (1783) was restated even more forcefully in the pages of his *The American Magazine* (1787–88) and was already forming the rationale of his *Dissertations on the English Language* (1789).

In this patriotic mood Webster undertook to revise and enlarge the third part of his *A Grammatical Institute of the English Language*. Entitled *An American Selection of Lessons in Reading and Speaking*, it was designed as a reader, to follow in the steps of the Speller (Part I) and the Grammar (Part II). That his schoolbooks were a principal medium for the transmission of Webster's patriotism was symbolically acknowledged by the presence of Mirabeau's advice on the title page of Webster's work: "Let the first word he lisps be Washington." No better indication of its nationalistic content is to be found than Webster's own statement in the book's preface:

In the choice of pieces, I have been attentive to the political interests of America. I consider it as a capital fault in all our schools that the books generally used contain subjects wholly uninteresting to our youth, while the writings that marked the revolution, which are not inferior in any respect to the orations of Cicero and Demosthenes and which are calculated to impress interesting truths upon young minds, lie neglected and forgotten. Several of those masterly addresses of Congress, written at the commencement of the late revolution, contain such noble sentiments of liberty and patriotism that I cannot help wishing to transfuse them into the breasts of the rising generation.

Among selections by leading patriots, including Benjamin Franklin and Joel Barlow, Webster introduced in *An American Selection of Lessons in Reading and Speaking* a number of his own essays, notably "Remarks on the Manners, Government, Laws, and Domestic Debt of America," which constitutes Selection Four. The title suggests Webster's ability to package a variety of the ills of young America and lay them at the doorstep of political and cultural disunion. In one of his most aggressive essays, Webster here attempts to instill in the youth of America his passionate desire for total independence, cautioning that "A revolution in the form of government is but a revolution in name unless attended with a change of principles and manners, which are the springs of government."

"... The Revolution ... Was but Just Begun"

A fundamental mistake of the Americans has been that they considered the revolution as completed when it was but just begun. Having laid the pillars of the building, they ceased to exert themselves, and seemed to forget that the whole superstructure was then to be erected. This country is independent in government, but totally dependent in manners, which are the basis of government. Men seem not to attend to the difference between Europe and America in point of age and improvement, and are disposed to rush with heedless emulation into an imitation of manners for which we are not prepared.

Every person tolerably well versed in history knows that nations are often compared to individuals and to vegetables in their progress from their origin to maturity and decay. The resemblance is striking and just. This progress is as certain in nations as in vegetables; it is as obvious and its cause more easily understood, in proportion as the secret springs of action in government are more easily explained than the mechanical principles of vegetation.

This progress, therefore, being assumed as a conceded fact, suggests a forcible argument against the introduction of European manners into America. The business of men in society is, first, to secure their persons and estates by arms and wholesome law, then to procure the conveniences of life by arts and labor; but it is in the last stages only of national improvement that luxury and amusements become public benefits, by dissipating accumulations of wealth and furnishing employment and food for the poor. And luxury then is not beneficial except when the wealth of a nation is wasted within itself. It is perhaps always true that an old civilized nation cannot, with propriety, be the model for an infant nation, either in morals, in manners or fashions, in literature, or in government.

A constant increase of wealth is ever followed with a multiplication of vices—this seems to be the destiny of human affairs—wisdom therefore directs us to retard, if possible, and not to accelerate the progress of corruption. But an introduction of the fashionable diversions of Europe into America is an acceleration of the growth of vices which are yet in their infancy, and an introduction of new ones too infamous to be mentioned. A dancing-school among the Tuscaroras is not a greater absurdity than a masquerade in America. A theatre under the best regulations is not essential to our public and private happiness. It may afford entertainment to individuals, but it is at the expense of private taste and public morals. The great misfortune of all exhibitions of this kind is this, that they reduce all taste to a level. Not only the vices of all classes of people are brought into view, but of all ages and nations. The intrigues of a nobleman and the scurrility of shoe-blacks are presented to the view of both sexes of all ages; the vices of the age of Elizabeth and of Charles II are recorded by the masterly pens of a Shakespear and a Congreve, and by repeated representation they are "hung on high," as the Poet expresses it, "to poison half mankind." The fact is that all characters must be presented upon a theatre, because all characters are spectators; and a nobleman and a sailor, a duchess and a washer-woman that attend constantly on the exhibitions of vice became equally depraved—their tastes will be nearly alike as to vice, the one is as prepared for a crime as the other. It is for this reason that many of the amusements of nations more depraved than ourselves are highly pernicious in this country. They carry us forward by hasty strides to the last stages of corruption, a period that every benevolent man will deprecate and endeavor to retard. This circumstance—the difference in the stages of our political existence—should make us shun the vices which may be polite and even necessary in older states, and endeavor to preserve our manners by being our own standards. By attaching ourselves to foreign manners we counteract the good effects of the revolution, or rather render them incomplete. A revolution in the form of government is but a revolution in name unless attended with a change of principles and manners, which are the springs of government.

We are now in a situation to answer all the purposes of the European nations: independent in government and dependent in manners. They give us their fashions, they direct *our* taste to make a market for *their* commodities, they engross the profits of our industry, without the hazard of defending us or the expence of supporting our civil government. A situation more favourable to *their* interest, or more repugnant to our *own*, they could not have chosen for us, nor *we* embraced.

If such is the state of facts and if the influence of foreign manners does actually defeat the purposes of the revolution, if our implicit submission to the prevailing taste of European courts involves individuals and the public in unnecessary expences, it is the power of a few influential characters in each of our commercial cities to remedy the whole evil. And in a reformation of this kind the ladies would have no inconsiderable share.

It is really a matter of astonishment that the pride of the Americans has so long submitted tamely to a foreign yoke. Aside of all regard to interest, we should expect that the idea of being a nation of apes would mortify minds accustomed to freedom of thought and would prompt them to spurn their chains.

Have the ladies in America no ingenuity, no taste? Do they not understand what dresses are most convenient and elegant, what modes are best adapted to the climate or other circumstances of this country? They most certainly do. Foreigners acknowledge that the native beauty and understanding of the American ladies are not excelled in any country and equalled in very few. And one would imagine that the modes of embellishing so many personal charms ought not, in all cases, to be prescribed by the milliners and mantua makers on the other side of the Atlantic.

When the gentlemen in America shall exercise spirit enough to be their own judges of taste in dress, when they have wisdom to consult the circumstances of this country and fortitude to retain a fashion as long as their *own interest* requires, instead of changing it when *other nations* direct, when the ladies shall exercise the right of their sex and say we will *give* the laws of fashion to our *own nation,* instead of *receiving* them from *another,* we will perform our part of the revolution. When both sexes shall take more pride and pleasure in being their own standards than in being humble imitators of those who riot on the profits of our commerce, we shall realize a new species of independence—an independence flattering to generous minds and more productive of wealth than all the laws of power or the little arts of national policy. And in this revolution of manners, there needs not [be] any sacrifice of real dress. I will venture to estimate that the retrenching of superfluous articles which constitute no part of dress and serve but to disfigure an elegant person—articles that are made and sent to us to support the six-penny day laborers of Europe—I say, a retrenching of those trifling articles only would be an annual saving to America sufficient to pay one half the interest of our federal debt. We can throw no blame on foreign nations; they are wise and profit by our want of spirit and taste.

On the footing that all mankind are brethren, perhaps it is generous in us to assist foreigners, who are a part of the Great Family.

It is to be wished, however, that we might first discharge our honest debts—that the soldier, whose labor and blood have purchased our empire and whose services have been paid with a shadow of reward, might be indemnified by the justice of his country; that the widow and orphan might at least receive the stipulated satisfaction for losses which money cannot repair. Yes, let us first be *just* and then *generous.* When we have no better use for our superfluous property, then let us bestow it upon our wretched brethren of the human race. They will repay our charity with gratitude and bless God that he has peopled one half the world with a race of freemen to enrich the tyrants and support the vassals of the other.

This same veneration for eminent foreigners and the bewitching charms of fashion have led the Americans to adopt the modern corruptions of our language. Very seldom have men examined the structure of the language to find reasons for their practice. The pronunciation and use of words have been subject to the same arbitrary or accidental changes as the shape of their garments. My lord wears a hat of certain size and shape; he pronounces a word in a certain manner; and both must be right, for he is a *fashionable* man. In Europe this is right in dress, and men who have not an opportunity of learning the just rules of our language are in some degree excusable for imitating those whom they consider as superiors. But in men of science this imitation can hardly be excused.

I presume we may safely say that our language has suffered more injurious changes in America since the British army landed on our shores than it had suffered before in the period of three centuries. The bucks and bloods tell us that there is no proper standard in language, that it is all arbitrary. The assertion, however, serves but to show their ignorance. There are in the language itself decisive reasons for preferring one pronunciation to another, and men of science should be acquainted with these reasons. But if there were none, and every thing rested on practice, we should never change a general practice without substantial reasons; no change should be introduced which is not an obvious improvement.

But our leading characters seem to pay no regard to rules or their former practice. To know and embrace every change made in Great Britain, whether right or wrong, is the extent of their enquiries and the height of their ambition. It is to this deference we may ascribe the long catalogue of errors in pronunciation and of false idioms which disfigure the language of our mighty fine speakers. And should this imitation continue, we shall be hurried down the stream of corruption with older nations, and our language, with theirs, be lost in an ocean of perpetual changes. The only hope we can entertain is that America, driven by the shock of a revolution from the rapidity of the current, may glide along near the margin with a gentler stream and sometimes be wafted back by an eddy.

It is perhaps a fundamental principle of government that men are influenced more by habit than by any abstract ideas of right and wrong. Few people examine into the propriety of particular usages or laws, or if they examine, few indeed are capable of comprehending their propriety. But every man knows what is a law or general practice, and he conforms to it not because it is right or best, but because it has been the practice. It is for this reason that habits of obedience should not be disturbed. There are perhaps in every government some laws and customs which, when examined on theoretical principles, will be found unjust and even impolitic. But if the people acquiesce in those laws and customs, if they are attached to them by habit, it is wrong in the legislature to attempt an innovation which shall alarm their apprehensions. There are multitudes of absurdities practised in society in which people are evidently happy. Arraign those absurdities before the tribunal of examination—people may be convinced of their impropriety, they may even be convinced that better schemes can be projected—and yet it might be impossible to unite their opinions so as to establish different maxims. On the other hand, there are many good institutions in which, however, there may be theoretical faults which, if called into public view and artfully represented, might shake the best government on earth.

Speculative philosophers and historians have often described, and sometimes ridiculed, the warmth with which nations have defended errors in religion and government. With the most profound deference for wise and respectable men, I must think they are guilty of a mistake, and that the errors which nations fight to defend exist only in the heads of these theorists. Whatever speculation may tell us, experience and the peace of society require us to consider every thing as right which a nation believes to be so. Every institution, every custom, may be deemed just and proper which does not produce inconveniences that the bulk of mankind can see and feel. The tranquility of society, therefore, should never be disturbed for a philosphical distinction.

It will perhaps be objected that these doctrines, if practised, would prevent all improvements in science, religion, and govern-

ment. By no means; but they point out the method in which all
improvements should be made when opinion and fixed habits are to
be overthrown or changed. They show that all reformation
should be left to the natural progress of society or to the conviction
of the mind. They show the hazard or impracticability of changes
before the minds of the body of the people are prepared for the
innovation. I speak not of despotic governments, where the will of
the prince is enforced by an army; and yet even absolute tyrants
have been assassinated for not attending to the spirit and habits of
their subjects.

In vain do rulers oppose the general opinion of the people. By
such opposition, Philip II of Spain kept one part of his subjects for
half a century butchering the other, and in the end lost one third of
his dominions. By not regarding the change of habits in the nation,
Charles I of England lost his head. By carrying his changes too far,
Cromwell began to oppose the spirit of the nation, and had he lived
to prosecute his system, that spirit would, in a few years, have
brought his neck to the block. The general spirit of the nation
restored to the throne the son of the prince whom that spirit had
but a few years before arraigned and condemned. By opposing that
spirit James was obliged to leave his kingdom, and the sense of the
nation still excludes the family which, by their own law of succes-
sion, has the best title to the throne. But there is no prescription
against general opinion, no right that can enter the list against the
sense of a nation—that sense which, after all our reasonings, will
for ever determine what is best.

The truth of these remarks is proved by examples in this
country. An immense revenue might have been drawn from
America without resistance in almost any method but that which
the British parliament adopted. But their first attempts were made
upon articles of common necessity—the attempts were too visible—
the people felt and resisted. Their apprehensions were alarmed
—their fears, whether well founded or imaginary, were multiplied
and confirmed by newspaper rhapsodies and finally produced a
combined opposition to all British taxation. Then Great Britain
should have compounded—she did not—she opposed the general
sense of two millions of her subjects, and lost the whole.

But a question will arise, how far may the people be opposed when their schemes are evidently pernicious? I answer, this can never happen thro' design, and errors even of the populace may gradually be removed. If the people cannot be convinced by reason and argument of the impolicy or injustice of a favorite scheme, we have only to wait for the consequences to produce conviction. All people are not capable of just reasoning on the great scale of politics, but all can feel the inconveniences of wrong measures, and evils of this kind generally furnish their own remedy. All popular legislatures are liable to great mistakes. Many of the acts of the American legislatures respecting money and commerce will, to future generations, appear incredible. After repeated experiments, people will be better informed and astonished that their fathers could make such blunders in legislation.

But let us attend to the immediate and necessary consequences of the American revolution.

So great an event as that of detaching millions of people from their parent nation could not have been effected without the operation of powerful causes. Nothing but a series of real or imaginary evils could have shaken the habits by which we were governed and produced a combined opposition against the power of Great Britain. I shall not enumerate any of these evils, but observe that such evils, by twenty years' operation upon the fears or feelings of the Americans, had alienated their affections or weakened those habits of respect by which we were predisposed to voluntary obedience. When a government has lost respect, it has lost the main pillar of its authority. Not even a military force can supply the want of respect among subjects. A change of sentiment prepares the way for a change of government, and when that change of sentiment had become general in America, nothing could have prevented a revolution.

But it is more easy to excite fears than to remove them. The jealousy raised in the minds of Americans against the British government wrought a revolution, but the spirit did not then subside—it changed its object, and by the arts of designing men, and the real distresses consequent on such a political storm, was directed against our own government. The restraints imposed by respect and habits of obedience were broken thro', and the licentious passions of men set afloat.

Nothing can be so fatal to morals and the peace of society as a violent shock given to public opinion or fixed habits. Polemic disputes have often destroyed the friendship of a church and filled it, not only with rancor, but with immorality. Public opinion, therefore, in religion and government, the great supports of society, should never be suddenly unhinged. The separation of America, however, from all dependence on European government could not have been effected without previously attacking and changing opinion. It was an essential step, but the effects of it will not easily be repaired. That independence of spirit which preceded the commencement of hostilities, and which victory has strengthened—that love of dominion, inherent in the mind of man, which our forms of government are continually flattering, that licentiousness of enquiry which a jealousy of rights first produced and still preserves—cannot be controuled and subdued but by a long series of prudent and vigorous measures.

Perhaps the present age will hardly see the restoration of perfect tranquility. But the spirit and principles which wrought our separation from Great Britain will mostly die with the present generation; the next generation will probably have new habits of obedience to our governments; and habits will govern them with very little support from law.

Most of the states had new constitutions of government to form; they had a kind of interregnum, an interval when respect for all government was suspended, an interval fatal in the last degree to morals and social confidence. This interval between the abolition of the old constitution and the formation of a new one lasted longer in Massachusetts than in the other states, and there the effects were most visible. But perhaps it is impossible to frame a constitution of government, in the closet, which will suit the people; for it is frequent to find one, the most perfect in theory, the most objectionable in practice. Hence we often hear popular complaints against the present governments in America, and yet these may proceed rather from the novelty of the obedience required than from any real errors or defects in the systems; it may be nothing but the want of habit which makes people uneasy—the same articles which now produce clamors and discontent may, after twenty years' practice, give perfect satisfaction. Nay, the same civil regulation which the present generation may raise a mob to resist, the next generation may raise a mob to defend.

But perhaps a more immediate and powerful cause of a corruption of social principles is a fluctuation of money. Few people seem to attend to the connection between money and morals; but it may doubtless be proved to the satisfaction of every reflecting mind that a sudden increase of specie in a country, and frequent and obvious changes of value, are more fruitful sources of corruption of morals than any events that take place in a community.

The first effect of too much money is to check manual labor, the only permanent source of wealth. Industry which secures subsistence and advances our interest by slow and regular gains is the best preservative of morals, for it keeps men employed and affords them few opportunities of taking unfair advantages. A regular commerce has nearly the same effect as agriculture or the mechanic arts, for the principles are generally fixed and understood.

Speculation has the contrary effect. As its calculations for profit depend on no fixed principles, but solely on the different value of articles in different parts of the country, or on accidental and sudden variations of value, it opens a field for the exercise of ingenuity in taking advantage of these circumstances.

But the speculators are not the only men whose character and principles are exposed by such a state of the currency; the honest laborer and the regular merchant are often tempted to forsake the established principles of advance. Every temptation of this kind attacks the moral principles and exposes men to small deviations from the rectitude of commutative justice.

Dissipation was another consequence of a flood of money. No country perhaps on earth can exhibit such a spirit of dissipation among men who derive their support from business as America. It is supposed by good judges that the expences of subsistence, dress, and equipage were nearly doubled in commercial towns the two first years after peace. I have no doubt the support of the common people was enhanced 25 per cent. This augmentation of expences, with a diminution of productive industry, are the consequences of too much money.

That instability of law to which republics are prone is another source of corruption. Multiplication and changes of law have a great effect in weakening the force of government by preventing or destroying habits. Law acquires force by a steady operation, and government acquires dignity and respect in proportion to the uniformity of its proceedings. Necessity perhaps has made our federal and provincial governments frequently shift their measures; and the unforseen or unavoidable variation of public securities, with the impossibility of commanding the resources of the continent to fulfil engagements, all predict a continuation of the evil. But the whole wisdom of legislatures should be exerted to devise a system of measures which may preclude the necessity of changes that tend to bring government into contempt.

Extensive credit in a popular government is always pernicious and may be fatal. When the people are deeply or generally involved, they have power and strong temptations to introduce an abolition of debts, an agrarian law, or that modern refinement on the Roman plan which is a substitute for both—a paper currency, issued on depreciating principles.

In governments like ours it is policy to make it the interest of people to be honest. In short, the whole art of governing consists in binding each individual by his particular interest to promote the aggregate interest of the community.

Laws to prevent credit would [be] beneficial to poor people. With respect to the contraction of debt, people at large in some measure resemble children: they are not judges even of their own interest. They anticipate their incomes, and very often, by miscalculation, much more than their incomes. But this is not the worst effect. An easy credit throws them off their guard in their expences. In general we observe that a slow, laborious acquisition of property creates a caution in expenditures, and gradually forms the miser. On the other hand, a sudden acquisition of money, either by gambling, lotteries, privateering, or marriage, has a tendency to open the heart, to throw the man off his guard, and thus make him prodigal in his expences. Perhaps this is ever the case, except when a penurious habit has been previously formed.

An easy and extensive credit has a similar effect. When people can possess themselves of property without previous labor, they consume it with improvident liberality. A prudent man will not; but a large proportion of mankind have not prudence and fortitude enough to resist the demands of pride and appetite. Thus they often riot on other men's property which they would not labor to procure. They form habits of indolence and extravagance which ruin their families and impoverish their creditors.

The only way to become rich at home and respectable abroad is to become industrious and to throw off our slavish dependence on foreign manners which obliges us to sacrifice our opinions, our taste, and our interest to the policy and aggrandisement of other nations.

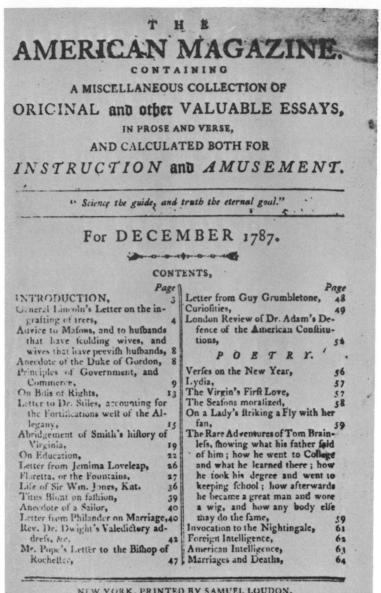

THE
AMERICAN MAGAZINE.

CONTAINING

A MISCELLANEOUS COLLECTION OF

ORIGINAL and other VALUABLE ESSAYS,

IN PROSE AND VERSE,

AND CALCULATED BOTH FOR

INSTRUCTION and *AMUSEMENT.*

" Science the guide, and truth the eternal goal."

For DECEMBER 1787.

CONTENTS,

NEW YORK, PRINTED BY SAMUEL LOUDON,
And sold by the PRINTER, by Messieurs BERRY and ROGERS, Mr. R.
HODGE, Mr. S. CAMPBELL, Mr. T. ALLEN, and Mr. T. GREENLEAF.

Front page from the first
issue of *The American Magazine,*
edited by Noah Webster.

"Americans, Unshackle Your Minds . . ."

From *The American Magazine,* 1787–88

EDITOR'S COMMENTS

Noah Webster has been called, with propriety, "Schoolmaster to America." Over and above his years as a practicing teacher and lecturer, founder of Amherst College, and author of immensely successful textbooks, there is a suggestion of the schoolmaster in all of Webster's works. Whether his subject is language or politics, finance or religion, one notes a consistent tenor of instruction in his essays. His extensive digressions into the historical background of these subjects are the work of a devoted pedagogue, carefully nurturing an adolescent culture from the front of the American classroom.

Eminence in learning was, from the beginning, a central part of Webster's vision of America, and his reflections on government confirmed education as a critical pillar of republican government. At one point he linked the "diffusion of knowledge" with the "general distribution of property" as the "immoveable basis" of liberty (see Selection Three, p. 58), and at another, in Part III of *Sketches of American Policy*, he termed public education "the firmest security of our liberties." This intimate relationship between education and liberty gave Webster his best opportunity to demonstrate the need for indigenous American institutions. On his tour in 1785–86 he delivered a series of lectures on the subject, published them in the first six issues of his *The American Magazine* a year later, and reprinted them in *A Collection of Essays and Fugitiv Writings* (1790). Though these views were modified in later years, particularly with regard to the value of classical study, they stand as an outstanding example of post-Revolutionary educational thought. Webster never surrendered his conviction that the broad diffusion of learning was vital to the maintenance of liberty and the promotion of American interests. His later work in the Massachusetts legislature, anticipating the successes of Horace Mann, attest Webster's fidelity to this conviction.

Webster's basic proposition that education should be adapted to the particular culture of a nation met with only limited contemporary approval. His belief that in a republican government special attention should be given to the development of political education found expression in Thomas Jefferson's University of Virginia, and the beginnings of the academy movement reflected a growing degree of support for Webster's opinion that facilities were needed for the preparation of youth in careers other than the established professions. But on one count—namely, his strong opposition to the exposure of youth to foreign study and travel—Webster had the almost universal support of national leaders. Washington and Jefferson were particularly vocal in their agreement, and it was their desire to offer a counterattraction to the seductive charms of Europe that led the two Presidents to urge the establishment of a national university, a proposal on which Webster appears to have been silent. Though all three men believed that a republic lived on learning, they joined in prescribing against foreign education, at least in the formative years, as detrimental to the development of national loyalties and sound morality.

"*Americans, Unshackle Your Minds . . .*"

The education of youth is, in all governments, an object of the first consequence. The impressions received in early life usually form the characters of individuals, a union of which forms the general character of a nation.

The mode of education and the arts taught to youth have, in every nation, been adapted to its particular stage of society or local circumstances.

In the martial ages of Greece, the principal study of its legislators was to acquaint the young men with the use of arms, to inspire them with an undaunted courage, and to form in the hearts of both sexes an invincible attachment to their country. Such was the effect of their regulations for these purposes that the very women of Sparta and Athens would reproach their own sons for surviving their companions who fell in the field of battle.

Among the warlike Sythians, every male was not only taught to use arms for attack and defence, but was obliged to sleep in the field, to carry heavy burthens, and to climb rocks and precipices in order to habituate himself to hardships, fatigue, and danger.

In Persia, during the flourishing reign of the great Cyrus, the education of youth, according to Zenophon, formed a principal branch of the regulations of the empire. The young men were divided into classes, each of which had some particular duties to perform, for which they were qualified by previous instructions and exercise.

While nations are in a barbarous state they have few wants and consequently few arts. Their principal objects are defence and subsistence; the education of a savage, therefore, extends little farther than to enable him to use, with dexterity, a bow and a tomahawk.

But in the progress of manners and of arts, war ceases to be the employment of whole nations; it becomes the business of a few, who are paid for defending their country. Artificial wants multiply the number of occupations, and these require a great diversity in the mode of education. Every youth must be instructed in the business by which he is to procure subsistence. Even the civilities of behavior, in polished society, become a science; a bow and a curtesy are taught with as much care and precision as the elements of mathematics. Education proceeds, therefore, by gradual advances from simplicity to corruption. Its first object among rude nations is safety; its next, utility; it afterwards extends to convenience; and among the opulent part of civilized nations it is directed principally to show and amusement.

In despotic states education, like religion, is made subservient to government. In some of the vast empires of Asia, children are always instructed in the occupation of their parents; thus the same arts are always continued in the same families. Such an institution cramps genius and limits the progress of national improvement; at the same time it is an almost immoveable barrier against the introduction of vice, luxury, faction, and changes in government. This is one of the principal causes which have operated in combining numerous millions of the human race under one form of government and preserving national tranquility for incredible periods of time. The empire of China, whose government was founded on the patriarchical discipline, has not suffered a revolution in laws, manners, or language for many thousand years.

In the complicated systems of government which are established among the civilized nations of Europe, education has less influence in forming a national character, but there is no state in which it has not an inseperable connection with morals and a consequential influence upon the peace and happiness of society.

Education is a subject which has been exhausted by the ablest writers, both among the ancients and moderns. I am not vain enough to suppose I can suggest any new ideas upon so trite a theme as education in general, but perhaps the manner of conducting the youth in America may be capable of some improvement. Our constitutions of civil government are not yet firmly established; our national character is not yet formed; and it is an object of vast magnitude that systems of education should be adopted and pursued which may not only diffuse a knowledge of the science, but may implant in the minds of the American youth the principles of virtue and of liberty, and inspire them with just and liberal ideas of government and with an inviolable attachment to their own country. It now becomes every American to examine the modes of education in Europe to see how far they are applicable in this country, and whether it is not possible to make some valuable alterations adapted to our local and political circumstances. Let us examine the subject in two views: first, as it respects arts and sciences; secondly, as it is connected with morals and government. In each of these articles let us see what errors may be found, and what improvements suggested, in our present practice.

The first error that I would mention is a too general attention to the dead languages, with a neglect of our own.

This practice proceeds probably from the common use of the Greek and Roman tongues before the English was brought to perfection. There was a long period of time when these languages were almost the only repositories of science in Europe. Men who had a taste for learning were under a necessity of recurring to the sources, the Greek and Roman authors. These will ever be held in the highest estimation both for style and sentiment, but the most valuable of them have English translations which, if they do not contain all the elegance, communicate all the ideas of the originals. The English language, perhaps, at this moment is the repository of as much learning as one half the languages of Europe. In copiousness it exceeds all modern tongues; and though inferior to the Greeks and French in softness and harmony, yet it exceeds the French in variety; it almost equals the Greek and Roman in energy, and falls very little short of any language in the regularity of its construction.[1]

In deliberating upon any plan of instruction, we should be attentive to its future influence and probable advantages. What advantage does a merchant, a mechanic, a farmer derive from an acquaintance with the Greek and Roman tongues? It is true the etymology of words cannot be well understood without a knowledge of the original languages of which ours is composed. But a very accurate knowledge of the meaning of words and of the true construction of sentences may be obtained by the help of dictionaries and good English writers, and this is all that is necessary in the common occupations of life. But suppose there is some advantage to be derived from an acquaintance with the dead languages; will this compensate for the loss of five or perhaps seven years of valuable time? Life is short, and every hour should be employed to good purposes. If there are no studies of more consequence to boys than those of Latin and Greek, let these languages employ their time; for idleness is the bane of youth. But when we have an elegant and copious language of our own, with innumerable writers upon ethics, geography, history, commerce, and government—subjects immediately interesting to every man—how can a parent be justified in keeping his son several years over rules of syntax which he forgets when he shuts his book or which, if remembered, can be of little or no use in any branch of business? This absurdity is the subject of common complaint—men see and feel the impropriety of the usual practice, and yet no arguments that have hitherto been used have been sufficient to change the system or to place an English school on a footing with a Latin one in point of reputation. It is not my wish to discountenance totally the study of the dead languages. On the other hand, I should urge a more close attention to them among young men who are designed for the learned professions. The poets, the orators, the philosophers, and the historians of Greece and Rome furnish the most excellent models of style and the richest treasures of science. The

---

[1] This remark is confined solely to its *construction*; in point of orthography, our language is intolerably irregular.

slight attention given to a few of these authors in our usual course of education is rather calculated to make pedants than scholars, and the time employed in gaining superficial knowledge is really wasted. "A little learning is a dangerous thing." "Drink deep, or taste not the Pierian Spring."

But my meaning is that the dead languages are not necessary for men of business—merchants, mechanics, planters, &c.—nor of utility sufficient to indemnify them for the expence of time and money which is requisite to acquire a tolerable acquaintance with the Greek and Roman authors. Merchants often have occasion for a knowledge of some foreign living language—as the French, the Italian, the Spanish, or the German—but men whose business is wholly domestic have little or no use for any language but their own, much less for languages known only in books.

There is one very necessary use of the Latin language which will always prevent it from falling into neglect, which is that it serves as a common interpreter among the learned of all nations and ages. Epitaphs, inscriptions on monuments and medals, treaties, &c., designed for perpetuity, are written in Latin, which is every where understood by the learned and, being a dead language, is liable to no change.

But the high estimation in which the learned languages have been held has discouraged a due attention to our own. People find themselves able without much study to write and speak the English intelligibly, and thus have been led to think rules of no utility. This opinion has produced various and arbitrary practices in the use of the language, even among men of the most information and accuracy; and this diversity has produced another opinion, both false and injurious to the language, that there are no rules or principles on which the pronunciation and construction can be settled.

This neglect is so general that there is scarcely an institution to be found in the country where the English tongue is taught regularly, from its elements to its true and elegant construction, in prose and verse. Perhaps in most schools boys are taught the definition of the parts of speech and a few hard names which they do not understand and which the teacher seldom attempts to explain—this is called *learning grammar*. This practice of learning questions and answers without acquiring any ideas has given rise to a common remark, that *grammar is a dry study;* and so is every other study which is prosecuted without improving the head or the heart. The study of geography is equally dry when the subject is not understood. But when grammar is taught by the help of visible objects, when children perceive that differences of words arise from differences in things, which they may learn at a very early period of life, the study becomes entertaining as well as improving. In general, when a study of any kind is tiresome to a person, it is a presumptive evidence that he does not make any proficiency in knowledge, and this is almost always the fault of the instructor.

In a few instances perhaps, the study of English is thought an object of consequence; but here also there is a great error in the common practice, for the study of English is preceded by several years' attention to Latin and Greek. Nay, there are men who contend that the best way to become acquainted with English is to learn Latin first. Common sense may justly fume at such an opinion, but experience proves it to be false.[2]

*   *   *

The only practicable method to reform mankind is to begin with children, to banish, if possible, from their company every low bred, drunken, immoral character. Virtue and vice will not grow together in a great degree, but they will grow where they are planted; and when one has taken root, it is not easily supplanted by the other. The great art of correcting mankind, therefore, consists in prepossessing the mind with good principles.

For this reason society requires that the education of youth should be watched with the most scrupulous attention. Education, in a great measure, forms the moral characters of men, and morals are the basis of government.[3] Education should therefore be the first care of a legislature—not merely the institution of schools, but the furnishing of them with the best men for teachers. A good system of education should be the first article in the code of politi-

---

[2] Webster's discussion has been abbreviated here.—Ed.
[3] *Plus ibi boni mores valent, quam alibi bona leves.* Tacitus *Der mar. germ.* xix.

cal regulations, for it is much easier to introduce and establish an effectual system for preserving morals than to correct, by penal statutes, the ill effects of a bad system. I am so fully persuaded of this that I shall almost adore that great man who shall change our practice and opinions and make it respectable for the first and best men to superintend the education of youth.

Another defect in our schools, which, since the revolution, is become inexcuseable, is the want of proper books. The collections which are now used consist of essays that respect foreign and ancient nations. The minds of youth are perpetually led to the history of Greece and Rome or to Great Britain—boys are constantly repeating the declamations of Demosthenes and Cicero or debates upon some political question in the British Parliament. These are excellent specimens of good sense, polished style, and perfect oratory; but they are not interesting to children. They cannot be very useful, except to young gentlemen who want them as models of reasoning and eloquence in the pulpit or at the bar.

But every child in America should be acquainted with his own country. He should read books that furnish him with ideas that will be useful to him in life and practice. As soon as he opens his lips he should rehearse the history of his own country—he should lisp the praises of liberty and of those illustrious heroes and statesmen who have wrought a revolution in his favor.

A selection of essays respecting the settlement and geography of America—the history of the late revolution and of the most remarkable characters and events that distinguished it—and a compendium of the principles of the federal and provincial governments should be the principal school book in the United States. These are interesting objects to every man—they call home the minds of youth and fix them upon the interests of their own country, and they assist in forming attachments to it, as well as in enlarging the understanding.

It is observed by the great Montesquieu that the laws of education ought to be relative to the principles of the government.

In despotic governments the people should have little or no education except what tends to inspire them with a servile fear. Information is fatal to despotism.

In monarchies education should be partial, and adapted to the rank of each class of citizens. But "in a republican government," says the same writer, "the whole power of education is required." Here every class of people should *know* and *love* the laws. This knowledge should be diffused by means of schools and newspapers, and an attachment to the laws may be formed by early impressions upon the mind.

Two regulations are essential to the continuance of republican governments: 1. Such a distribution of lands and such principles of descent and alienation as shall give every citizen a power of acquiring what his industry merits; 2. Such a system of education as gives every citizen an opportunity of acquiring knowledge and fitting himself for places of trust. These are fundamental articles—the *sine qua non* of the existence of the American republics.

Hence the absurdity of our copying the manners and adopting the institutions of monarchies.

In several states we find laws passed establishing provision for colleges and academies where people of property may educate their sons, but no provision is made for instructing the poorer rank of people even in reading and writing. Yet in these same states every citizen who is worth a few shillings annually is entitled to vote for legislators. This appears to me a most glaring solecism in government. The constitutions are *republican*, and the laws of education are *monarchical*. The *former* extend civil rights to every honest industrious man; the *latter* deprive a large proportion of the citizens of a most valuable privilege.

In our American republics, where government is in the hands of the people, knowledge should be universally diffused by means of public schools. Of such consequence is it to society that the people who make laws should be well informed that I conceive no legislature can be justified in neglecting proper establishments for this purpose.

When I speak of a diffusion of knowledge, I do not mean

merely a knowledge of spelling books & the New Testament. An acquaintance with ethics and with the general principles of law, commerce, money, and government is necessary for the yeomanry of a republican state. This acquaintance they might obtain by means of books calculated for schools and read by the children during the winter months, and by the circulation of public papers.

"In Rome it was the common exercise of boys at school to learn the laws of the twelve tables by heart, as they did their poets and classic authors." (Middleton's life of Cicero, I, 14.)

What an excellent practice this [is] in a free government!

It is said—indeed, by many—that our common people are already too well informed. Strange paradox! The truth is they have too much knowledge and spirit to resign their share in government, and are not sufficiently informed to govern themselves in all cases of difficulty.

There are some acts of the American legislatures which astonish men of information—and blunders in legislation are frequently ascribed to bad intentions. But if we examine the men who compose these legislatures, we shall find that wrong measures generally proceed from ignorance, either in the men themselves or in their constituents. They often mistake their own interest because they do not foresee the remote consequences of a measure.

It may be true that all men cannot be legislators, but the more generally knowledge is diffused among the substantial yeomanry, the more perfect will be the laws of a republican state.

Every small district should be furnished with a school at least four months in a year, when boys are not otherwise employed. This school should be kept by the most reputable and well-informed man in the district. Here children should be taught the usual branches of learning—submission to superiors and to laws, the moral or social duties, the history and transactions of their own country, the principles of liberty and government. Here the rough manners of the wilderness should be softened and the principles of virtue and good behaviour inculcated. The *virtues* of men are of more consequence to society than their abilities, and for this reason the *heart* should be cultivated with more assiduity than the *head*.

Such a general system of education is neither impracticable nor difficult; and, excepting the formation of a federal government that shall be efficient and permanent, it demands the first attention of American patriots. Until such a system shall be adopted and pursued—until the statesman and divine shall write their efforts in *forming* the human mind, rather than in lopping its excrescences after it has been neglected, until legislators discover that the only way to make good citizens and subjects is to nourish them from infancy, and until parents shall be convinced that the *worst* of men are not the proper teachers to make the *best*—mankind cannot know to what degree of perfection society and government may be carried. America affords the fairest opportunities for making the experiment and opens the most encouraging prospect of success.

Before I quit this subject, I beg leave to make some remarks on a practice which appears to be attended with important consequences: I mean that of sending boys to Europe for an education, or sending to Europe for teachers. That this was right before the revolution will not be disputed, at least so far as national attachments were concerned, but the propriety of it ceased with our political relation to Great Britain.

In the first place, our honor as an independent nation is concerned in the establishment of literary institutions adequate to all our own purposes, without sending our youth abroad or depending on other nations for books and instructors. It is very little to the reputation of America to have it said abroad that after the heroic achievements of the late war this independent people are obliged to send to Europe for men and books to teach their children A B C.

But in another point of view, a foreign education is directly opposite to our political interests and ought to be discountenanced, if not prohibited.

Every person of common observation will grant that most men prefer the manners and the government of that country where they are educated. Let ten American youths be sent each to a different European kingdom and live there from the age of twelve to twenty, & each will give the preference to the country where he has resided.

The period from twelve to twenty is the most important in life. The impressions made before that period are commonly effaced; those that are made during that period *always* remain for many years, and *generally* thro' life.

Ninety-nine persons of a hundred who pass that period in England or France will prefer the people, their manners, their laws, and their government to those of their native country. Such attachments are injurious both to the happiness of the men and to the political interests of their own country. As to private happiness, it is universally known how much pain a man suffers by a change of habits in living. The customs of Europe are and ought to be different from ours, but when a man has been bred in one country, his attachments to its manners make them, in a great measure, necessary to his happiness; on changing his residence he must therefore break his former habits, which is always a painful sacrifice; or the discordance between the manners of his own country and his habits must give him incessant uneasiness; or he must introduce into a circle of his friends the manners in which he was educated. All these consequences may follow at the same time, and the last, which is inevitable, is a public injury. The refinement of manners in every country should keep pace exactly with the increase of its wealth—and perhaps the greatest evil America now feels is an improvement of taste and manners which its wealth cannot support.

A foreign education is the very source of this evil—it gives young gentlemen of fortune a relish for manners and amusements which are not suited to this country; which, however, when introduced by this class of people, will always become fashionable.

But a corruption of manners is not the sole objection of a foreign education: an attachment to a *foreign* government, or rather a want of attachment to our *own*, is the natural effect of a residence abroad during the period of youth. It is recorded of one of the Greek cities that in a treaty with their conquerors it was required that they should give a certain number of *male children* as hostages for the fulfilment of their engagements. The Greeks absolutely refused, on the principle that these children would imbibe the ideas and embrace the manners of foreigners or lose their love for their own country. But they offered the same number of *old* men without hesitation. This anecdote is full of good sense. A man should always form his habits and attachments in the country where he is to reside for life. When these habits are formed, young men may travel without danger of losing their patriotism. A boy who lives in England from twelve to twenty will be an *Englishman* in his manners and his feelings; but let him remain at home till he is twenty and form his attachments, he may then be several years abroad and still be an *American*.[4] There may be exceptions to this observation, but living examples may be mentioned to prove the truth of the general principle here advanced respecting the influence of habit.

It may be said that foreign universities furnish much better opportunities of improvement in the sciences than the American. This may be true, and yet will not justify the practice of sending young lads from their own country. There are some branches of science which may be studied to much greater advantage in Europe than in America, particularly chymistry. When these are to be acquired, young gentlemen ought to spare no pains to attend the best professors. It may, therefore, be useful in some cases for students to cross the Atlantic to *complete* a course of studies, but it is not necessary for them to go early in life nor to continue a long time. Such instances need not be frequent even now, and the necessity for them will diminish in proportion to the future advancement of literature in America.

It is, however, much questioned whether, in the ordinary course of study, a young man can enjoy greater advantages in Europe than in America. Experience inclines me to raise a doubt whether the danger to which a youth must be exposed among the sons of dissipation abroad will not turn the scale in favor of our American colleges. Certain it is that four fifths of the great literary characters in America never crossed the Atlantic.

[4] Webster's citations of authority have been omitted.—Ed.

But if our universities and schools are not so good as the English or Scotch, it is the business of our rulers to improve them—not to endow them merely, for endowments alone will never make a flourishing seminary, but to furnish them with professors of the first abilities and most assiduous application and with a complete apparatus for establishing theories by experiments. Nature has been profuse to the Americans in genius and in the advantages of climate and soil. If this country, therefore, should long be indebted to Europe for opportunities of acquiring any branch of science in perfection, it must be by means of a criminal neglect of its inhabitants.

The difference in the nature of the American and European governments is another objection to a foreign education. Men form modes of reasoning or habits of thinking on political subjects in the country where they are bred; these modes of reasoning may be founded on fact in all countries, but the same principles will not apply in all governments because of the infinite variety of national opinions and habits. Before a man can be a good legislator, he must be intimately acquainted with the temper of the people to be governed. No man can be thus acquainted with a people without residing amongst them and mingling with all companies. For want of this acquaintance a Turgot and a Price may reason most absurdly upon the constitutions of the American states; and when any person has been long accustomed to believe in the propriety or impropriety of certain maxims or regulations of government, it is very difficult to change his opinions or to persuade him to adapt his reasoning to new and different circumstances.

One half of the European Protestants will now contend that the Roman Catholic religion is subversive of civil government. Tradition, books, education have concurred to fix this belief in their minds, and they will not resign their opinions even in America, where some of the highest civil offices are in the hands of Roman Catholics.

It is, therefore, of infinite importance that those who direct the councils of a nation should be educated in that nation. Not that they should restrict their personal acquaintance to their own country, but their first ideas, attachments, and habits should be acquired in the country which they are to govern and defend. When a knowledge of their own country is obtained and an attachment to its laws and interests deeply fixed in their hearts, then young gentlemen may travel with infinite advantage and perfect safety. I wish not, there, to discourage traveling, but, if possible, to render it more useful to individuals and to the community. My meaning is that *men* should travel, and not *boys*.

But it is time for the Americans to change their usual route and travel thro a country which they never think of, or think beneath their notice. I mean the United States.

While these states were a part of the British Empire, our interest, our feelings, were those of Englishmen—our dependence led us to respect and imitate their manners and to look up to them for our opinions. We little thought of any national interest in America; and while our commerce and governments were in the hands of our parent country and we had no common interest, we little thought of improving our acquaintance with each other or of removing prejudices & reconciling the discordant feelings of the inhabitants of different provinces. But independence and union render it necessary that the citizens of different states should know each other's characters and circumstances, that all jealousies should be removed, that mutual respect and confidence should succeed, and a harmony of views and interests be cultivated by a friendly intercourse.

A tour thro the United States ought now to be considered as a necessary part of a liberal education. Instead of sending young gentlemen to Europe to view curiosities and learn vices and follies, let them spend twelve or eighteen months in examining the local situation of the different states—the rivers, the soil, the population, the improvements and commercial advantages of the whole, with an attention to the spirit and manners of the inhabitants, their laws, local customs, and institutions. Such a tour should at least precede a tour to Europe, for nothing can be more ridiculous than a man traveling in a foreign country for information when he can give no account of his own. When, therefore, young gentlemen have finished an academic education, let them travel thro America, and afterwards to Europe, if their time and fortunes will permit. But if they cannot make the tour thro both, that in America is certainly to be preferred; for the people of America, with all their information, are yet extremely ignorant of the geography, policy, and manners of their neighbouring states. Except a few gentlemen whose public employments in the army and in Congress have extended their knowledge of America, the people in this country, even of the higher classes, have not so correct information respecting the United States as they have respecting England or France. Such ignorance is not only disgraceful, but is materially prejudicial to our political friendship and federal operations.

Americans, unshackle your minds and act like independent beings. You have been children long enough, subject to the control, and subservient to the interest, of a haughty parent. You have now an interest of your own to augment and defend—you have an empire to raise and support by your exertions, and a national character to establish and extend by your wisdom and virtues. To effect these great objects, it is necessary to frame a liberal plan of policy and build it on a broad system of education. Before this system can be formed and embraced, the Americans must *believe* and *act* from the belief that it is dishonorable to waste life in mimicking the follies of other nations and basking in the sunshine of foreign glory.

"*Now* Is the Time and *This* the Country . . ."

From the Appendix to *Dissertations on the English Language*, 1789

EDITOR'S COMMENTS

One of Webster's most diverting excursions into the study of language was his attempt to reform English spelling. The accompanying selection suggests the enthusiasm with which the young editor briefly pursued this reform, encouraged by the aging Ben Franklin, to whom Webster dedicated his *Dissertations on the English Language.*

Essentially, spelling reform was for Webster a short-lived excursion. In 1783 he had made caustic reference to "pedantic" writers who attempted "expunging the superfluous letters," observing with schoolmasterly propriety that: "Our language is indeed pronounced very differently from the spelling. This is an inconvenience we regret, but cannot remedy. To attempt a progressive change is idle; it will keep the language in perpetual fluctuation. . . . We may better labour to speak our language with propriety and elegance, as we have it, than to attempt a reformation without advantage or probability of success." This is to be compared with amusement to the following quotation from the preface to Webster's *A Collection of Essays and Fugitiv Writings,* published in 1790: "There iz no alternativ. Every possible reezon that could ever be offered for altering the spelling of wurds stil exists in full force; and if a gradual reform should not be made in our language, it will proov that we are less under the influence of reezon than our ancestors."

Greater maturity and reflection led, as the later selections in this volume attest, to a much more moderate form of orthographic reform. In the preface to *An American Dictionary of the English Language,* Webster was again the schoolmaster, admonishing that "dabbling spirit of innovation" that was "perpetually disturbing" the regularity of the English language. Nonetheless, to Webster must go great credit for the disappearance of the superfluous "k" from "public" and "u" from "honor," as well as for the consistent use of the ending "-er" in "center," "theater," etc., and other spellings now established in American usage.

The accompanying selection, taken from the appendix to Webster's *Dissertations on the English Language,* is presented, however, more for its exposition of the *rationale* of reform than for its commentary upon the need for change, and more for the manner of effecting change than for the nature of that change. It illustrates the extent to which Webster sought to purge the American language of English habit, its closing lines underscoring his confidence not only that an awakened spirit of independence was abroad in the United States, but that experimental reform would *here* and *now* find fertile soil in which to take root.

"Now *Is the Time and* This *the Country . . .*"

It has been observed by all writers on the English language that the orthography or spelling of words is very irregular, the same letters often representing different sounds and the same sounds often expressed by different letters. For this irregularity two principal causes may be assigned:

1. The changes to which the pronunciation of a language is liable from the progress of science and civilization;

2. The mixture of different languages occasioned by revolutions in England or by a predilection of the learned for words of foreign growth and ancient origin.

To the first cause may be ascribed the difference between the spelling and pronunciation of Saxon words. The northern nations of Europe originally spoke much in gutturals. This is evident from the number of aspirates and guttural letters which still remain in the orthography of words derived from those nations and from the modern pronunciation of the collateral branches of the Teutonic: the Dutch, Scotch, and German. Thus *k* before *n* was once pronounced as in *knave, know;* the *gh* in *might, though, daughter,* and other similar words; the *g* in *reign, feign,* &c.

But as savages proceed in forming languages they lose the guttural sounds in some measure and adopt the use of labials and the more open vowels. The ease of speaking facilitates this progress, and the pronunciation of words is softened in proportion to a national refinement of manners. This will account for the difference between the ancient and modern languages of France, Spain, and

Italy, and for the difference between the soft pronunciation of the present languages of those countries and the more harsh and guttural pronunciation of the northern inhabitants of Europe.

In this progress the English have lost the sounds of most of the guttural letters. The *k* before *n* in *know*, the *g* in *reign* and in many other words are become mute in practice; and the *gh* is softened into the sound of *f* as in *laugh* or is silent as in *brought*.

To this practice of softening the sounds of letters, or wholly suppressing those which are harsh and disagreeable, may be added a popular tendency to abbreviate words of common use. Thus *Southwark*, by a habit of quick pronunciation, is become *Suthark*; *Worcester* and *Leicester* are become *Wooster* and *Lester*; *business*, *bizness*; *colonel*, *curnel*; *cannot*, *will not*, *cant*, *wont*.[1] In this manner the final *e* is not heard in many modern words in which it formerly made a syllable. The words *clothes*, *cares*, and most others of the same kind were formerly pronounced in two syllables.[2]

Of the other cause of irregularity in the spelling of our language I have treated sufficiently in the first dissertation. It is here necessary only to remark that when words have been introduced from a foreign language into the English, they have generally retained the orthography of the original, however ill adapted to express the English pronunciation. Thus *fatigue, marine, chaise* retain their French dress, while, to represent the true pronunciation in English, they should be spelt *fateeg, mareen, shaze*. Thus thro an ambition to exhibit the etymology of words, the English in *Philip, physic, character, chorus*, and other Greek derivatives preserve the representatives of the original Φ and X; yet these words are pronounced, and ought ever to have been spelt, *Fillip, fyzzic* or *fizzic, karacter, korus*.[3]

---

[1] WONT is strictly a contraction of *woll not*, as the word was anciently pronounced.

[2] "Ta-ke, ma-ke, o-ne, bo-ne, sto-ne, wil-le, &c. dissyllaba olim fuerunt quae nunc habenter pro monosyllabis."—Wallis.

[3] The words *number, chamber*, and many others in English are from the French *nombre, chambre*, &c. Why was the spelling changed or, rather, why is the spelling of *lustre, metre, theatre, not* changed? The cases are precisely similar. The Englishman who first wrote *number* for *nombre* had no greater authority to make the change than any modern writer has to spell *lustre, metre* in a similar

But such is the state of our language. The pronunciation of the words which are strictly *English* has been gradually changing for ages, and since the revival of science in Europe the language has received a vast accession of words from other languages, many of which retain an orthography very ill suited to exhibit the true pronunciation.

The question now occurs: ought the Americans to retain these faults which produce innumerable conveniences in the acquisition and use of the language, or ought they at once to reform these abuses and introduce order and regularity into the orthography of the AMERICAN TONGUE?

Let us consider this subject with some attention.

Several attempts were formerly made in England to rectify the orthography of the language.[4] But I apprehend their schemes failed of success rather on account of their intrinsic difficulties than on account of any necessary impracticability of a reform. It was proposed in most of these schemes not merely to throw out superfluous and silent letters, but to introduce a number of new characters. Any attempt on such a plan must undoubtedly prove unsuccessful. It is not to be expected that an orthography perfectly regular and simple, such as would be formed by a "Synod of Grammarians on principles of science," will be substituted for that confused mode of spelling which is now established. But it is apprehended that great improvements may be made and an orthography almost regular, or such as shall obviate most of the present difficulties with little trouble and opposition.

The principal alterations necessary to render our orthography sufficiently regular and easy are these:

1. The omission of all superfluous or silent letters, as *a* in *bread*. Thus *bread, head, give, breast, built, meant, realm, friend* would

---

manner, *luster, meter*. The change in the first instance was a valuable one; it conformed the spelling to the pronunciation, and I have taken the liberty in all my writings to pursue the principle in *luster, meter, miter, theater, sepulcher*, &c.

[4] The first by Sir Thomas Smith, Secretary of State to Queen Elizabeth; another by Dr. Gill, a celebrated master of St. Paul's school in London; another by Mr. Charles Butler, who went so far as to print his book in his proposed orthography; several in the time of Charles the First; and in the present age, Mr. Elphinstone has published a treatise in a very ridiculous orthography.

be spelt *bred, hed, giv, brest, bilt, ment, relm, frend.* Would this alteration produce any inconvenience, any embarrassment or expense? By no means. On the other hand, it would lessen the trouble of writing and, much more, of learning the language; it would reduce the true pronunciation to a certainty; and while it would assist foreigners and our own children in acquiring the language, it would render the pronunciation uniform in different parts of the country and almost prevent the possibility of changes.

2. A substitution of a character that has a certain definite sound for one that is more vague and indeterminate. Thus by putting *ee* instead of *ea* or *ie,* the words *mean, near, speak, grieve, zeal* would become *meen, neer, speek, greev, zeel.* This alteration could not occasion a moment's trouble; at the same time it would prevent a doubt respecting the pronunciation, whereas the *ea* and *ie,* having different sounds, may give a learner much difficulty. Thus *greef* should be substituted for *grief, kee* for *key, beleev* for *believe, laf* for *laugh, dawter* for *daughter, plow* for *plough, tuf* for *tough, proov* for *prove, blud* for *blood,* and *draft* for *draught.* In this manner *ch* in Greek derivatives should be changed into *k,* for the English *ch* has a soft sound, as in *cherish,* but *k* always a hard sound. Therefore *character, chorus, cholic, architecture* should be written *karacter, korus, kolic, arkitecture;* and were they thus written, no person could mistake their true pronunciation.

Thus *ch* in French derivatives should be changed into *sh; machine, chaise, chevalier* should be written *masheen, shaze, shevaleer;* and *pique, tour, oblique* should be written *peek, toor, obleek.*

3. A trifling alteration in a character or the addition of a point would distinguish different sounds without the substitution of a new character. Thus a very small stroke across *th* would distinguish its two sounds. A point over a vowel in this manner, *ȧ* or *ȯ* or *ī,* might answer all the purposes of different letters. And for the dipthong *ow,* let the two letters be united by a small stroke, or both engraven on the same piece of metal with the left-hand line of the *w* united to the *o.*

These, with a few other inconsiderable alterations, would answer every purpose and render the orthography sufficiently correct and regular.

The advantages to be derived from these alterations are numerous, great, and permanent.

1. The simplicity of the orthography would facilitate the learning of the language. It is now the work of years for children to learn to spell; and after all, the business is rarely accomplished. A few men who are bred to some business that requires constant exercise in writing finally learn to spell most words without hesitation; but most people remain, all their lives, imperfect masters of spelling and liable to make mistakes whenever they take up a pen to write a short note. Nay, many people, even of education and fashion, never attempt to write a letter without frequently consulting a dictionary.

But with the proposed orthography a child would learn to spell without trouble in a very short time, and, the orthography being very regular, he would ever afterwards find it difficult to make a mistake. It would, in that case, be as difficult to spell *wrong* as it is now to spell *right*.

Besides this advantage, foreigners would be able to acquire the pronunciation of English, which is now so difficult and embarrassing that they are either wholly discouraged on the first attempt or obliged, after many years' labor, to rest contented with an imperfect knowledge of the subject.

2. A correct orthography would render the pronunciation of the language as uniform as the spelling in books. A general uniformity thro the United States would be the event of such a reformation as I am here recommending. All persons of every rank would speak with some degree of precision and uniformity.[5] Such a uniformity in these states is very desirable; it would remove prejudice and conciliate mutual affection and respect.

3. Such a reform would diminish the number of letters about one sixteenth or eighteenth. This would save a page in eighteen;

---

[5] I once heard Dr. Franklin remark "that those people spell best who do not know how to spell"; that is, they spell as their ears dictate, without being guided by rules, and thus fall into a regular orthography.

and a saving of an eighteenth in the expense of books is an advantage that should not be overlooked.

4. But a capital advantage of this reform in these states would be that it would make a difference between the English orthography and the American. This will startle those who have not attended to the subject, but I am confident that such an event is an object of vast political consequence. For the alteration, however small, would encourage the publication of books in our own country. It would render it, in some measure, necessary that all books should be printed in America. The English would never copy our orthography for their own use, and consequently the same impressions of books would not answer for both countries. The inhabitants of the present generation would read the English impressions, but posterity, being taught a different spelling, would prefer the American orthography.

Besides this, a *national language* is a band of *national union*. Every engine should be employed to render the people of this country *national*, to call their attachments home to their own country, and to inspire them with the pride of national character. However they may boast of independence and the freedom of their government, yet their *opinions* are not sufficiently independent; an astonishing respect for the arts and literature of their parent country and a blind imitation of its manners are still prevalent among the Americans. Thus an habitual respect for another country, deserved indeed and once laudable, turns their attention from their own interests and prevents their respecting themselves.

OBJECTIONS

1. "This reform of the alphabet would oblige people to relearn the language or it could not be introduced."

But the alterations proposed are so few and so simple that an hour's attention would enable any person to read the new orthography with facility, and a week's practice would render it so familiar that a person would write it without hesitation or mistake. Would this small inconvenience prevent its adoption? Would not the numerous national and literary advantages resulting from the change induce Americans to make so inconsiderable a sacrifice of time and attention? I am persuaded they would.

But it would not be necessary that men advanced beyond the middle stage of life should be at the pains to learn the proposed orthography. They would, without inconvenience, continue to use the present. They would read the *new* orthography without difficulty, but they would write in the *old*. To men thus advanced, and even to the present generation in general if they should not wish to trouble themselves with a change, the reformation would be almost a matter of indifference. It would be sufficient that children should be taught the new orthography, and that as fast as they come upon the stage, they should be furnished with books in the American spelling. The progress of printing would be proportioned to the demand for books among the rising generation. This progressive introduction of the scheme would be extremely easy; children would learn the proposed orthography more easily than they would the old, and the present generation would not be troubled with the change, so that none but the obstinate and capricious could raise objections or make any opposition. The change would be so inconsiderable and made on such simple principles that a column in each newspaper printed in the new spelling would, in six months, familiarize most people to the change, show the advantages of it, and imperceptibly remove their objections. The only steps necessary to ensure success in the attempt to introduce this reform would be a resolution of Congress ordering all their acts to be engrossed in the new orthography and recommending the plan to the several universities in America, and also a resolution of the universities to encourage and support it. The printers would begin the reformation by publishing short paragraphs and small tracts in the new orthography, school books would first be published in the same, curiosity would excite attention to it, and men would be gradually reconciled to the plan.

2. "This change would render our present books useless."

This objection is, in some measure, answered under the foregoing head. The truth is, it would not have this effect. The difference of orthography would not render books printed in one illegible to persons acquainted only with the other. The difference would not be so great as between the orthography of Chaucer and of the present age, yet Chaucer's works are still read with ease.

3. "This reformation would injure the language by obscuring etymology."

This objection is unfounded. In general, it is not true that the change would obscure etymology; in a few instances it might, but it would rather restore the etymology of many words; and if it were true that the change would obscure it, this would be no objection to the reformation.

It will perhaps surprize my readers to be told that in many particular words the modern spelling is less correct than the ancient. Yet this is a truth that reflects dishonor on our modern refiners of the language. Chaucer, four hundred years ago, wrote *bilder* for *builder, dedly* for *deadly, ernest* for *earnest, erly* for *early, brest* for *breast, hed* for *head,* and certainly his spelling was the most agreeable to the pronunciation.[6] Sidney wrote *bin, examin, sutable,* with perfect propriety. Dr. Middleton wrote *explane, genuin, revele,* which is the most easy and correct orthography of such words, and also *luster, theater* for *lustre, theatre.* In these and many other instances the modern spelling is a corruption, so that, allowing many improvements to have been made in orthography within a century or two, we must acknowledge also that many corruptions have been introduced.

In answer to the objection that a change of orthography would obscure etymology, I would remark that the etymology of most words is already lost even to the learned, and to the unlearned etymology is never known. Where is the man that can trace back our English words to the elementary radicals? In a few instances the student has been able to reach the primitive roots of words, but I presume the radicals of one tenth of the words in our language have never yet been discovered even by Junius, Skinner, or any other etymologist. Any man may look into Johnson or Ash and

---

[6] In Chaucer's life, prefixed to the edition of his works 1602, I find *move* and *prove* spelt almost correctly, *moove* and *proove.*

find that *flesh* is derived from the Saxon *floce, child* from *cild, flood* from *flod, lad* from *leode,* and *loaf* from *laf* or *hlaf.* But this discovery will answer no other purpose than to show that within a few hundred years the spelling of some words has been a little changed. We should still be at a vast distance from the primitive roots.

In many instances indeed, etymology will assist the learned in understanding the composition and true sense of a word, and it throws much light upon the progress of language. But the true sense of a complex term is not always, nor generally, to be learnt from the sense of the primitives or elementary words. The current meaning of a word depends on its use in a nation. This true sense is to be obtained by attending to good authors, to dictionaries, and to practice rather than to derivation. The former *must* be *right;* the latter *may* lead us into *error.*

But to prove of how little consequence a knowledge of etymology is to most people, let me mention a few words. The word *sincere* is derived from the Latin *sine cera,* "without wax," and thus it came to denote *purity of mind.* I am confident that not a man in a thousand ever suspected this to be the origin of the word; yet all men that have any knowledge of our language use the word in its true sense and understand its customary meaning as well as Junius did, or any other etymologist.

Yea or *yes* is derived from the imperative of a verb *avoir,* "to have," as the word is now spelt. It signifies therefore *have,* or *possess,* or *take* what you ask. But does this explication assist us in using the word? And does not every countryman who labors in the field understand and use the word with as much precision as the profoundest philosophers?

The word *temper* is derived from an old root *tem,* which signified *water.* It was borrowed from the act of *cooling* or moderating heat. Hence the meaning of *temperate, temperance,* and all the ramifications of the original stock. But does this help us to the modern current sense of these words? By no means. It leads us to understand the formation of languages and in what manner an idea of a visible action gives rise to a correspondent abstract idea; or, rather, how a word, from a literal and direct sense, may be applied to express a variety of figurative and collateral ideas. Yet the customary sense of the word is known by practice and as well understood by an illiterate man of tolerable capacity as by men of science.

The word *always* is compounded of *all* and *ways;* it had originally no reference to time, and the etymology or composition of the word would only lead us into error. The true meaning of words is that which a nation in general annex to them. Etymology, therefore, is of no use but to the learned; and for them it will still be preserved, so far as it is now understood, in dictionaries and other books that treat of this particular subject.

4. "The distinction between words of different meanings and similar sound would be destroyed."

"That distinction," to answer in the words of the great Franklin, "is already destroyed in pronunciation." Does not every man pronounced *all* and *awl* precisely alike? And does the sameness of sound ever lead a hearer into a mistake? Does not the construction render the distinction easy and intelligible the moment the words of the sentence are heard? Is the word *knew* ever mistaken for *new,* even in the rapidity of pronouncing an animated oration? Was *peace* ever mistaken for *piece, pray* for *prey, flour* for *flower?* Never, I presume, is this similarity of sound the occasion of mistakes.

If, therefore, an identity of *sound,* even in rapid speaking, produces no inconvenience, how much less would an identity of *spelling,* when the eye would have leisure to survey the construction? But experience, the criterion of truth, which has removed the objection in the first case, will also assist us in forming our opinion in the last.

There are many words in our language which, with the *same orthography,* have *two* or more *distinct meanings.* The word *wind,* whether it signifies *to move round* or *air in motion,* has the *same spelling;* it exhibits no distinction on the *eye* of a silent reader, and yet its meaning is never mistaken. The construction shows at sight in which sense the word is to be understood. *Hail* is used as an expression of joy or to signify frozen drops of water falling from the clouds. *Rear* is to raise up or it signifies the hinder part of an army. *Lot* signifies fortune or destiny, a plot of ground, or a certain proportion or share; and yet does this diversity, this contrariety of meanings, ever occasion the least difficulty in the ordinary language of books? It cannot be maintained. This diversity is found in all languages,[7] and altho it may be considered as a defect and occasion some trouble for foreign learners, yet to natives it produces no sensible inconvenience.

5. "It is idle to conform the orthography of words to the pronounciation, because the latter is continually changing."

This is one of Dr. Johnson's objections, and it is very unworthy of his judgment. So far is this circumstance from being a real objection that it is alone a sufficient reason for the change of spelling. On his principle of *fixing the orthography* while the *pronunciation is changing*, any *spoken language* must, in time, lose all relation to the *written language*; that is, the sounds of words would have no affinity with the letters that compose them. In some instances this is now the case, and no mortal would suspect from the spelling that *neighbour, wrought* are pronounced *nabur, rawt*. On this principle, Dr. Johnson ought to have gone back some centuries and given us, in his dictionary, the primitive Saxon orthography: *wol* for *will*, *ydilness* for *idleness*, *eyen* for *eyes*, *eche* for *each*, &c. Nay, he should have gone as far as possible into antiquity and, regardless of the changes of pronunciation, given us the primitive radical language in its purity. Happily for the language, that doctrine did not prevail till his time; the spelling of words changed with the pronunciation. To these changes we are indebted for numberless improvements, and it is hoped that the progress of them, in conformity with the national practice of speaking, will not be obstructed by the erroneous opinion even of Dr. Johnson. How much more rational is the opinion of Dr. Franklin, who says, "the orthography of our language began to be

---

[7] In the Roman language *liber* had four or five different meanings; it signified *free*, *the inward bark of a tree*, *a book*, sometimes *an epistle*, and also *generous*.

fixed too soon." If the pronunciation must vary from age to age (and some trifling changes of language will always be taking place), common sense would dictate a correspondent change of spelling. Admit Johnson's principles, take his pedantic orthography for the standard, let it be closely adhered to in the future, and the flow changes in the pronunciation of our national tongue will in time make as great a difference between our *written* and *spoken* language as there is between the pronunciation of the present English and German. The *spelling* will be no more a guide to the pronunciation than the orthography of the German or Greek. This event is actually taking place, in consequence of the stupid opinion advanced by Johnson and other writers, and generally embraced by the nation.

All these objections appear to me of very inconsiderable weight when opposed to the great, substantial, and permanent advantages to be derived from a regular national orthography.

Sensible I am how much easier it is to *propose* improvements than to *introduce* them. Everything *new* starts the idea of difficulty; and yet it is often mere novelty that excites the appearance, for on a slight examination of the proposal the difficulty vanishes. When we firmly *believe* a scheme to be practicable, the work is *half* accomplished. We are more frequently deterred by fear from making an attack than repulsed in the encounter.

Habit also is opposed to changes, for it renders even our errors dear to us. Having surmounted all difficulties in childhood, we forget the labor, the fatigue, and the perplexity we suffered in the attempt, and imagin the progress of our studies to have been smooth and easy.[8] What seems intrinsically right is so merely thro habit.

Indolence is another obstacle to improvements. The most arduous

[8] Thus most people suppose the present mode of spelling to be really the *easiest* and *best*. This opinion is derived from habit; the new mode of spelling proposed would save three fourths of the labor now bestowed in learning to write our language. A child would learn to spell as well in one year as he can now in four. This is not a supposition, it is an assertion capable of proof; and yet people, never knowing or having forgot the labor of learning, suppose the present mode to be the easiest. No person but one who has taught children has any idea of the difficulty of learning to spell and pronounce our language in its present form.

task a reformer has to execute is to make people *think*, to rouse them from that lethargy which, like the mantle of sleep, covers them in repose and contentment.

But America is in a situation the most favorable for great reformations, and the present time is in a singular degree auspicious. The minds of men in this country have been awakened. New scenes have been for many years presenting new occasions for exertion; unexpected distresses have called forth the powers of invention; and the application of new expedients has demanded every possible exercise of wisdom and talents. Attention is roused, the mind expanded, and the intellectual facilities invigorated. Here men are prepared to receive improvements which would be rejected by nations whose habits have not been shaken by similar events.

Now is the time and *this* the country in which we may expect success in attempting changes favorable to language, science, and government. Delay in the plan here proposed may be fatal; under a tranquil general government the minds of men may again sink into indolence; a national acquiescence in error will follow, and posterity be doomed to struggle with difficulties which time and accident will perpetually multiply.

Let us then seize the present moment and establish a *national language* as well as a national government. Let us remember that there is a certain respect due to the opinions of other nations. As an independent people our reputation abroad demands that in all things we should be federal, be *national*; for if we do not respect *ourselves*, we may be assured that *other nations* will not respect us. In short, let it be impressed upon the mind of every American that to neglect the means of commanding respect abroad is treason against the character and dignity of a brave, independent people.

"... Americans Are Yet in Their Leading-Strings ..."

From *Ten Letters to Dr. Priestley*, 1800

EDITOR'S COMMENTS

When in 1794 the distinguished English chemist and dissenter Dr. Joseph Priestley arrived in the United States to spend his remaining years in the exile of Pennsylvania's Northumberland County "backwoods," he was greeted with mixed emotions. The vitriol of William Cobbett, writing under the name of "Peter Porcupine," was in marked contrast to the elaborate compliments of the Republican clubs and the newly founded Tammany Hall, suggesting a strong political division of opinion regarding the desirability of Priestley's immigration. It was immediately apparent that controversy had followed the scientist across the ocean.

Priestley's obvious and outspoken Republican sentiments made Webster, then living in the privacy of his New Haven home, more than ordinarily sensitive to the chemist's uncomplimentary observations on American culture, which appeared in 1799 in a pamphlet entitled *Letters to the Inhabitants of Northumberland*. These comments, presented ostensibly as a defense against the attacks of Cobbett, reflected Priestley's views of American life after five years' residence, and he expressed to Jefferson the hope that they might be of service "to the common cause."[1] Disillusioned at this juncture by the self-indulgence of Federalist partisans, Webster had no stomach for the acidity of Cobbett, and he denounced him to Priestley as an Anglophile from whom the "Old Whigs . . . have withdrawn their patronage." Nonetheless, his enthusiasm for the ideal of a strong America was sufficiently intense so that he could hardly resist framing a reply to Priestley's veiled suggestion that the ideal was far short of realization. Thus, in

[1] April 10, 1801, in E. F. Smith, *Priestley in America, 1794–1804* (Philadelphia: P. Blakiston's Son & Co., 1920), p. 123.

1800 he penned a hasty series of ten letters of rebuttal to the Northumberland critic.

The accompanying selection, taken from the ninth and tenth letters, provides a valuable and unusually reliable insight into the state of culture in the United States, or at least in the New England states, at the turn of the century. Notably at variance with the exaggerated claims of America's struggling institutions of higher learning, the letters contain a frank concession of intellectual inferiority by one who would have preferred to be able to give a better report of the condition of American culture. Webster's confidence that the potential for ultimate eminence reposed in the American nation remains amply clear nonetheless. His conception of education as a function of society is restated with clarity, particularly in reference to the prominence of political study in American education; and, as in many of his writings, Webster again stresses the economic foundation of cultural advancement, observing that "science demands leisure and money."

"... *Americans Are Yet in Their Leading-Strings* ..."

Sir,

Two pamphlets of your writing addressed to the inhabitants of Northumberland, by accident falling into my hands, have excited no small degree of surprize and appear to merit a few comments. I had before thought that no man of ordinary reading could be so little acquainted with the state of public mind in the United States as you appear to be. You say you *see* almost all the newspapers in Philadelphia; it is to be wished, Sir, that you would *learn* the opinions of the inhabitants of New England before you assert things that have not the least foundation.

In your maxims of political arithmetic, republished from the *Aurora*, are found some assertions and opinions not altogether correct, although many of your observations are, I confess, too well founded.

I agree with you fully that our colleges are disgracefully destitute of books and philosophical apparatus, and that a duty on books without discrimination is highly impolitic. Very many of the best authors cannot be printed in the United States for half a century or more, and I am ashamed to own that scarcely a branch of science can be fully investigated in America for want of books, especially original works. This defect of our libraries I have experienced myself in searching for materials for the *History of Epidemic Diseases*.

In regard to the state of learning in general, your remarks are not sufficiently discriminating. You say there is "less knowledge in

America than in most of the countries of Europe." The truth seems
to be that in the eastern states knowledge is more diffused among
the laboring people than in any country on the globe. The learning
of the people extends to a knowledge of their own tongue, of
writing and arithmetic sufficient to keep their own simple accounts;
they read not only the Bible and newspapers, but almost all read
the best English authors, as the *Spectator, Rambler,* and the works
of Watts, Doderidge, and many others. If you can find any country in Europe where this is done to the same extent as in New
England, I am very ill informed.

But in the higher branches of literature our learning is superficial
to a shameful degree. Perhaps I ought to except the science of law,
which, being the road to political life, is probably as well understood as in Great Britain; and ethics and political science have been
greatly cultivated since the American Revolution. On political
subjects, I have no hesitation in saying that I believe the learning
of our eminent statesmen to be superior to that of most European
writers, and their opinions far more correct. They have all the
authors on these subjects, united with much experience which no
European country can have had. This has enabled our statesmen to
correct many of the theories which lead astray European writers.

But as to classical learning, history, civil and ecclesiastical,
mathematics, astronomy, chymistry, botany, and natural history—
excepting here and there a rare instance of a man who is eminent in
some one of these branches—we may be said to have no learning at
all, or a mere smattering. And what is more distressing to me, I see
every where a disposition to decry the study of ancient and original
authors, which I deem far superior to the moderns and from which
the best modern writers have drawn the finest parts of their
productions.

There is another circumstance still more afflictive to a man who
is attached, as I am, to a republican government, and one that I
perceive has not occurred to you. This is, that the equal distribution
of estates and the small property of our citizens—both of which
seem connected with our form of government, if not essential to
it—actually tend to depress the sciences. Science demands leisure

and money. Our citizens have property only to give their sons a
four years' education—a time scarcely sufficient to give them a
relish for learning and far inadequate to wide and profound researches. As soon as a young man has closed this period of study,
and while he is at the beginning of the alphabet of science, he must
betake himself to a profession, he must hurry through a few
books—which, by the way, are rarely original works, but compila-
tions and abridgements—and then must enter upon practice and get
his living as well as he can. And as to libraries, we have no such
things. There are not more than three or four tolerable libraries in
America, and these are extremely imperfect. Great numbers of the
most valuable authors have not found their way across the Atlantic.

But if our young men had more time to read, their estates will
not enable them to purchase the books requisite to make a learned
man—and this inconvenience, resulting from our government and
the state of society, I know not how to remedy. As this, however, is
the government to which you are attached, you will certainly do us
a great service if you can devise a plan for avoiding its disadvantages. And I can further inform you that any application to
legislatures for money will be unsuccessful. The utmost we can do
is to squeeze a little money occasionally from the public treasuries
to furnish buildings and a professor or two. But as to libraries,
public or private, men who do not understand their value will be
the last to furnish the means of procuring them. Besides, our rage
for gain absorbs all other considerations—science is a secondary
object, and a man who has grown suddenly from a dunghill by a
fortunate throw of the die avoids a man of learning as you would a
tiger. There are exceptions to this remark, and some men of taste,
here and there scattered over our country, adorn the sciences and
the moral virtues.

The Americans want only the *means* of improvement—their
genius and industry are no where exceeded. The mechanical inventions of the Americans testify to the powers of their genius, and the
distinction enjoyed in Europe by several American artists, while it
is an honor to the country where the encouragement is found, is an
evidence that the human race do not degenerate in the western

world. Opportunity, means, patronage alone are wanting to raise
the character of this country to an eminent rank among nations.

––––––––––

If the Americans are yet in their leading-strings as to some parts
of literature, there is the more room for improvement, and I am
confident that the genius of my fellow citizens will not be slack in
the important work. You will please to recollect, Sir, that during
one hundred and sixty years of our childhood we were in our
nonage, respecting our parent and looking up to her for books,
science, and improvements. From her we borrowed much learning
and some prejudices, which time alone can remove. And be assured, Dr. Priestley, that the parent is yet to derive some scientific
improvements from the child. Some false theories, some errors in
science, which the British nation has imbibed from illustrious men
and nourished from an implicit reliance on their authority, are to be
prostrated by the penetrating genius of America.

And after all, Sir, let candor confess that something has been
done in the New World which reflects honor on its inhabitants. A
wilderness converted into a garden and clothed with fruitful fields;
many hundred miles of country covered with handsome towns and
cities; numerous bridges and roads that equal those of the best
improved parts of Europe; numerous inventions in mechanic arts
and some in other branches of science; a number of the first artists
in Europe, with a few eminent philosophers; and, were it not for
offending you, I would add a commerce extended to the remotest
corners of the globe—are evidences of at least a small portion of
genius and a great deal of industry. If you will name any free
country, or indeed any country, where the half has been done in
the same time, I will confess my ignorance of the state of the
world. The experiment alone by which it has been decided that a
government can be framed and put into operation by free deliberation and consent of the people, independent of artifice or violence,
is the most precious tribute that mankind can receive from the New
World, and ought of itself to rescue the character of its inhabitants
from the imputation of dulness or barbarism.

"Nothing Is So Fatal to Truth and Tranquillity . . ."

From the Preface to *Miscellaneous Papers on Political and Commercial Subjects*, 1802

EDITOR'S COMMENTS

As in so many matters of national concern, Webster shared Washington's view against partisanship in politics. He saw in the emerging political clubs evidence of militant factionalism that could eventually rend the spirit and frustrate the ideal of union. As early as 1789, in dedicating his *Dissertations on the English Language* to Franklin, Webster had praised the elder statesman for being "violently attached to no political party" and for laboring "to reconcile contending factions in government." Increasingly thereafter, Webster sought to emulate Franklin by seeking out and attacking those who promoted partisanship.

As a Federalist, of course, Webster loosed upon the party and person of Jefferson his most violent criticism. His "Address to the President of the United States on the Subject of His Administration," published in *Miscellaneous Papers on Political and Commercial Subjects* (1802), is a model of intemperate criticism, although it does contain one of the earliest and most effective criticisms of the spoils system, with which Webster had had immediate experience in New Haven. In fairness, it must be said that his "Letter to General Hamilton, occasioned by his Letter to President Adams," written two years earlier, demonstrates Webster's impartial distaste for political partisanship. Both letters, however, are fine examples of what Henry Jones Ford has called "the tone of extreme rage that dishonors the political contention of the period."[1]

The accompanying selection, from the preface to Webster's *Miscellaneous Papers on Political and Commercial Subjects,* is a lucid statement of the "Old Federalist" view of parties, though it betrays the au-

[1] Henry Jones Ford, *Washington and His Colleagues* (New Haven: Yale University Press, 1918), pp. 173–74.

thor's greater dislike for one party than for the other. Depicting the Federalists as "men of principle" forced to unite in opposition to the selfish designs of the Republicans, Webster reveals his assumption that men of high character with a strong sense of union can reconcile all the varied interests and conflicting aspirations of the emerging nation. The preface embellishes, in some detail, the central objection to parties—namely, that "to be divided is to be ruined"—and visits a plague of righteous indignation upon both the Republican and Federalist houses.

Webster's alarm over "the turbulence of the democratic spirit" reflects his strong anti-French sentiment, which began during an unpleasant evening with the notorious Citizen Genêt in 1793 and accelerated with his research into the French Revolution. In the pages of the *American Minerva* and in his *The Revolution in France* (1794) he warned his fellow citizens, "Americans! Be not deluded. In seeking *liberty*, France has gone beyond her." With this violent objection to the excesses of French Jacobinism, as well as an undiscriminating tendency to attribute similar objectives to American Republicans, Webster started down the road to political disillusion and oblivion. By the time the accompanying selection appeared, Webster was liable to periods of profound discouragement, in which he could write to a friend that he had "no hope for the duration of the Union."[2]

[2] Letter to Samuel Bayard, March 2, 1802, in Warfel, *Letters of Noah Webster*, p. 250.

"*Nothing Is So Fatal to Truth and Tranquillity . . .*"

No task is more delicate and hazardous than that of criticism and censure. To err is the common lot of men; to acknowledge errors is the rare felicity of great minds. The man who discovers his own mistake feels dissatisfied with himself; he who exposes the mistakes of another incurs his displeasure. Yet in political affairs, in which the individuals of a society have a common interest, it is the right and even the duty of every citizen who believes public measures to be wrong to express his opinions with decency and candor, and offer the reasons on which they are founded.

Nothing is so fatal to truth and tranquillity as party spirit. It is rash, imperious, unyielding, unforgiving. Blind to truth and deaf to argument, it sees no merit in an enemy, no demerit in a friend. Urged by the passion or convenience of the moment, it rushes impetuously to the attainment of its object regardless of events and forgetting that its own example may be drawn into precedent and, under a change of parties, prove a two-edged sword, as fatal to friends as to foes.

To a man versed in the history of nations, the condition of parties in the United States presents nothing new but the men and the forms of proceeding. The general principles, views, and passions displayed are the same as have characterized parties in all ages and countries. Individuals of aspiring minds who have been mortified by neglect or irritated by the agitations of successless competition, men who can neither bear an equal nor yield to a superior, have the address to inlist into their service the credulous and illiterate multitude. To oppose them men of principle unite and form a party. Public measures are proposed or attacked with zeal, opposition begets obstinacy, argument is resisted by will, mutual concessions are either not proposed or rejected, and laws passed under such circumstances are either soon repealed or ineffectual in their operation.

Parties thus arrayed against each other often lose sight of the original points of difference or magnify trifling differences into matters of vast concern to the public. Zeal is inflamed to enthusiasm, the regard to truth is extinguished in the desire of victory, and moderation yields to the apprehension of defeat. Then begins the reign of corruption—each party determines to triumph, and neither constitution nor law, religion nor morality, reputation nor conscience, can raise effectual barriers to restrain their passions and pursuits.

In this warfare of parties, the adherents to each voluntarily put themselves under a favorite *leader* and take a popular *name*. Thus organized, each party rallies under the *name* and the *leader* with the *esprit du corps* for the moving principle, forgetting the origin, or ignorant of the motives, of the association. The leader is stimulated by pride; his adherents, by the sound of his name or the appellation of the party, which is neither understood nor intelligible. A white rose, a red rose, a cockade, round-head or cavalier, whig or tory, federalist or democrat, or other insignificant appellation becomes the rallying point for a headstrong populace, prepared for violence.

In the effervescence of popular passions, the leader who has gained the confidence of a party must feed the hopes and gratify the expectations of his adherents. Applying to faction the military maxim of M. Porcius Cato, *Bellum se ipsum alit,* "War feeds itself," a victorious leader supplies the wants, and secures the attachment, of his followers by dividing among them the spoils of the vanquished. Then commences the reign of persecution and revenge. The man who mounts into office on popular confidence may rise with impunity above the constitution of his country and trample on the rights of the people. Under the specious titles of a *republican* and the *friend of the people* he may exercise the despotism of a Frederic.

To parties in government or religion may be applied the profound remark of the Roman historian respecting the populace: "They are distinguished for mean servility or insolent domination; real liberty, which occupies a middle station between extremes, they can neither enjoy nor reject with moderation."[3] Nor is it less true, as the historian adds, that "demagogues are seldom wanting who favor the passions of the people and inflame their restless and unruly dispositions to the horrid work of blood and slaughter." The men who flatter the people become their masters, and the party which, while a minority, will lick the dust to gain the ascendancy becomes, in power, insolent, vindictive, and tyrannical.

However surprising may be the fact, the truth of it is not to be questioned that parties equally forget or spurn the maxims of prudence by which individuals regulate their conduct. In political concerns, *expedience,* rather than strict theoretical justice, is the rule of action and the measure of practicable good. Yet how rarely will parties yield an iota of their pretensions to meet their opponents on the ground of *expedience!* The federalists in 1798 stood on high ground—they pushed their advantages too far and contributed not a little to their own overthrow and to the triumph of men whose principles threaten a speedy dissolution of the Union.

The proclamation of neutrality in April, 1793, was advised by the policy, and sanctioned by the deliberate approbation, of the federal councils, while their opposers, with shameful solicitude, urged for the adoption of measures which would result in a war, in concert with France, against Great Britain. In 1798, when the outrages of the French government had turned the popular current, the federalists became the advocates of war, in direct contradiction of the principles of 1793, and nearly succeeded in carrying the propostion. In the period preceding 1797 the federalists complained, and justly, of the influence which the French had obtained

---

[3] *Aut servit humiliter, aut superbe dominatur—libertatem quae media est, nec epernere modice, nec habere sciunt.* Livy *Lib.* xxiv. 25.

over American presses; but in 1797, when a professed British subject and a declared enemy of our independence established a Gazette in Philadelphia, the federalists opened not their mouths, but in many places gave him unusual encouragement. Anterior to the year 1798 the federalists were outrageously clamorous against every opposer of the executive authority, denouncing him as a jacobin and disorganizer; but the moment the President adopted a measure that displeased particular men, the federalists turned their arms against the administration. And in the pursuit of this absurd policy, if one of their friends, wishing to be consistent and foreseeing the ruinous tendency of such measures, happened to call in question the propriety of these contradictory proceedings, they fell upon him like wild beasts, ready to tear him in pieces.

Of the measures before mentioned, we now severely feel the effects. The following essay on the Rights of Neutral Nations presents to view another subject no less interesting; and the consequences of the principles admitted by our government in regard to it are not yet fully felt and may be remote. The Congress which conducted the revolution recognized, with general approbation, the principles of the "Armed Neutrality" in regard to the freedom of neutral ships, and the proclamation of neutrality in 1793 virtually acknowledged the principles in recommending the "modern usage of nations" as the rule of contraband commerce. Yet in the treaty with Great Britain the administration receded from the principles. Then, to vindicate the conduct of the government, immense efforts were made to prove the claims of neutral nations ill-founded and to lessen the importance of free ships during a war. The *immediate* effect of these efforts has been to give a false coloring to the subject and a wrong direction to the public opinion. The *ultimate* effect, by enabling the British court in future negociations to repel our claims to the principle of free ships, by the reasoning of our own administration, and the very popular administration of General Washington, no man can undertake to predict nor to estimate. The writer himself was misled by his confidence in the executive and in the elementary authors to which the appeal was made for authorities. But the public should be disabused of their errors. Within a year past an effort has been made, thro the medium of the public prints, to depreciate the principles of free ships; and one writer has attempted to persuade our citizens that the privilege is not only no benefit, but a positive evil to a neutral nation. Where there is a contradiction there must be error. The unalterable principles of justice and true policy should not be held at the mercy of temporary attachments and averversons [aversions?].

Such are the mistakes of the federalists which have furnished their opposers with the most efficacious means of victory. On the other hand, the party which have assumed the name of *republican* have not only objected to federal measures of a wrong or equivocal tendency, but have opposed with unabating zeal the most salutary regulations. They have struggled to defeat the measures intended to establish public credit, to enforce the laws, and to secure a peace with Great Britain. They have execrated, and would have invoked fire from heaven to consume the proud but rich, learned, and respectable nation to which the world is greatly indebted for arresting the career of French victories. They have omitted no opportunity to weaken the administration of our government and degrade the honor of the American name. No public character, however pure, has been safe from the shafts of their malice; no corner of the United States has escaped the poison of their slanders.

Unfavorable as has been the opinion of the writer respecting the principles and views of the leading men in the party, he had no conception that a man in the United States would have been found weak enough to avow the principles on which the present administration has proceeded, nor bold enough, under cover of republican principles, to attack the most essential provisions of the national compact.

In this condition of things, when the domineering spirit of party frowns on moderation as apostacy or cowardice, who are the men to listen to truth and impartial discussion? Who will hazard the opprobrium of both parties to expose their mistakes and attempt to arrest the career of men whose intemperate zeal has pushed our affairs to this alarming crisis?

Let it be considered that nothing is more injurious to a cause than to attempt to defend what is not susceptible of defense. The advocate who dwells on a weak point exhausts his own powers, while he tires the patience, and impairs the confidence, of his judges. By insisting on every thing, a party often loses every thing. This is especially true in political affairs, where numerous interests are to be consulted and numerous opinions to be reconciled to a common result. If men would withdraw their attachment from systems and names, the sober, reflecting, unambitious citizens of both parties would, at this moment, coalesce on every measure essential to the public safety. If, instead of enlisting under the standard of *federalism* and *republicanism,* they would investigate principles and understand the true interests of the United States, the great body of people would unite in their conclusions. If the charm of names cannot be dissolved, our condition is hopeless. The supporters of the present administration, more especially in the southern states, are not all jacobins nor disorganizers. Great numbers of respectable men abandoned the late administration because they believed the government had abandoned the primary objects of the revolution and made improper concessions to the British government. Of this fact there is certain evidence. Their opinion is probably not correct in the latitude in which it is entertained, but it is not to be denied that some measures gave countenance to it. Both parties have committed errors—the true policy of our country unquestionably lies between the extremes of their measures. The federalists, as a party, appear to have the most correct ideas of government—ideas drawn from a view of the nature of man and from the history of society—and experiment will ultimately decide in their favor. At the same time, they have pushed their measures farther than the temper of the people will bear; and the writer believes that, in their honest zeal to preserve peace with Great Britain and a revenue undiminished, they have made some unnecessary concessions to the British government in regard to a neutral commerce in time of war.

The present ruling party, on the other hand, led astray by closet theories, are making experiments in government which all history and the observations of every day demonstrate to be idle and futile. Their principles are incompatible with the safety of society, and their administration disdains all constitutional obstacles to the accomplishment of their schemes. The consequences of such a system, pursued to its extent, are more easily imagined than described.

To avert the evils that threaten our public tranquility, more temper and forbearance, with a mutual disposition to conciliate confidence, must be manifested by the respective parties. Whatever may be the fact with regard to the precise degree of merit in their systems, it is prudent for both to recede from some of their pretensions. There is no exact standard of political right and wrong by which discordant opinions can in all cases be adjusted. Even the Constitution is not sufficiently explicit to furnish this standard. Our substitute for such a common arbiter must be found in mutual concessions which will answer the purpose, for it is a remark on which great stress is laid that *harmony of councils will obviate the errors and defects of legislation.* Mutual concessions, therefore, would be honorable to the parties—they are due to truth—they are demanded by the imperious voice of public duty and national safety. Nor is it to be questioned that, without receding from some of the ground which has been taken, the most upright and able men in our country will find it extremely difficult to recover the influence which they have lost and which they certainly deserve.

It is morally impossible that the body of a people can be enemies to public happiness. They may be, and often are, misled; yet in every case of this kind the evil will find a remedy in the inconveniences resulting from their councils. It is the remark of an accurate observer of human nature "that a few men only have discernment enough to distinguish in speculation what is expedient and useful from what is improper and pernicious; most men are taught only by experience."[4] Experience alone can convince the great mass of people of their mistake, and for the effect of experiment we must wait with patience. It is worse than useless to rail at men for being

---

[4] *Pauci prudentia, honesta ab deterioribus, utilia ab noxiis, discernunt; plures aliorum eventis docentur.* Tacitus *An. lib.* iv. 33.

in an error or for being misled. Instead of weakening their confidence in their leaders or convincing them of their mistake, personal ill treatment serves to confirm them; and resentment coming in aid of a natural attachment to a preconceived opinion renders the possessor incorrigible.

This impolitic conduct often multiplies the foes of a good cause without necessity and widens a breach which a temperate policy would strive to heal. If a man cannot assent to every measure of *his party*, he is abused and his reputation slandered, perhaps, too, by the very men who clamor most bitterly against the same conduct in their opposers. The man's pride and independence of mind revolt at the indignity, which he is conscious he does not deserve; resentment stimulates him to vindicate his principles and, finally, to abandon his persecutors. This mistaken policy of erecting a particular system of measures as an idol and chastizing every man who will not fall down and worship it has accelerated the overthrow of the federal interest—in one state it has been the most fruitful source of opposition to that interest—nor is there any party or cause which this species of overbearing persecution would not gradually fritter away and destroy.

Triumphant jacobinism in any country is a formidable calamity, overwhelming all good order, all social security, and all improvement in promiscuous ruin. But jacobinism is a monster which devours her own offspring. No nation of jacobins can exist, nor can a race of such monsters long tyrannize over a nation. The reign of error, of vice, of folly and passion must ever be short in proportion as it is violent and distructive.

The turbulence of the democratic spirit is a violent disease, incident to free states. France has felt the full force of its pangs, but the crisis is past and she is convalescent. Whether the United States are to suffer all the violence of the disease or only its milder symptoms, time only can determine. One thing is obvious—the present state of inflammation will not bear stimulant applications.

If arguments will not restrain the intemperate zeal and vindictive spirit of men in power, menaces and provocations will only serve to irritate that spirit. Nor will it be of any use to hold up to view the terrors of civil war. Foreign danger, indeed, would call for more passion, but internal dissensions call for less. No internal disputes should unsheath the sword—that should be reserved exclusively for defense against a foreign foe. A constitution prostrated, the independence of the judiciary destroyed, a revenue defrauded, offices committed to worthless men—these would be severe national calamities, but infinitely less evil than a drawn sword. Let rash heads be suspected—let violent hands be restrained —let public evils be left to operate on our citizens till they have learnt the cause and are willing to apply a peaceable remedy. As sure as the revolutions of day and night, the pernicious effects of a bad system of measures will alarm the fears and open the eyes of its advocates, provided the passions of the people can be liberated from the influence of hasty councils and guarded from the exasperations of headstrong men. The people can neither be *forced* nor *provoked* to renounce their errors. Nine tenths of the blood that has been shed in civil commotions would have been spared if a few ambitious leaders had been restrained until the people could have had time to pause and deliberate.

Amidst the angry passions of parties the writer has hitherto preserved that independence of mind without which man is no better than a machine. His opinions, except on the point before mentioned, have been uniform from the year 1793, when parties began to assume their present complexion. In 1795 he defended the conduct of our government in regard to neutral commerce; on this subject a more careful investigation has compelled him to change his opinion.

". . . To Dissolve the Charm of Veneration for Foreign Authorities . . ."

From the Preface to *A Compendious Dictionary of the English Language*, 1806

EDITOR'S COMMENTS

Webster was interested in words and their definitions throughout his adult life, although he was forty-eight years old and an established figure before the appearance of his first dictionary, the preface to which constitutes the accompanying selection. Large sections of his political and other essays are devoted to defining terms with a care that must have exasperated his opponents and dismayed even his supporters.[1] So great was Webster's preoccupation with the meaning of words, and so widely known, that a political satirist of the period could ridicule it as early as 1801. Leonard Chester put this line into the mouth of his caricature of John Trumbull: "I believe I must touch up brother Noah —no that won't do either, if he should get angry, he'll oppose my favorite scheme of augmenting the number of judges of the superior court, and come into the house and spend three days on the word *augmentation.*"[2]

This natural inclination to define words was given room to grow when Webster made his significant move from the cramped political arena in New York to the intellectual groves of New Haven. Equipped for the first time with the necessary financial means, Webster devoted almost full time to his literary pursuits, even recommending them to other vexed and discouraged politicians.[3] He found this work congenial to his personal tastes and integral to his ambitions for a greater America.

[1] See, for example, his definitions of the word "aristocracy" in *The Revolution in France, Considered in Respect to Its Progress and Effects* (New York: Bunce and Co., 1794), p. 49, and in the appendix to *Ten Letters to Dr. Priestley* (1800).

[2] Leonard Chester, *Federalism Triumphant in the Steady Habits of Connecticut Alone, or, The Turnpike Road to a Fortune. A comic opera or political farce in six acts* . . . (n.p., 1802).

[3] July 6, 1807, in Warfel, *Letters of Noah Webster*, p. 277.

Shortly after his *A Compendious Dictionary of the English Language* appeared, Webster wrote Joel Barlow that American dependence on English standards had put *"an end to inquiry,"* with the result that even the colleges had *"no spirit of investigation."*[4] Webster erected the small 1806 dictionary as a temporary breastwork against the extension of this crippling influence, meanwhile devoting himself to the "work of vast labor" that was to form a permanent bulwark. Though greeted on both sides of the Atlantic with derision and contempt as a vain and presumptuous effort, this dictionary was followed in the same year by a one-dollar abridgment, designed for school use, and by announcements that the intrepid Webster was proceeding with plans for a "complete" dictionary.

The accompanying selection demonstrates how readily dictionary-making fell into the rationale of Webster's entire career. To break the "chains of illusion" was as important as parting the fetter of political bondage, to be self-reliant in language was as vital to American strength as the avoidance of international alliances; for, as Webster wrote Barlow, American dependence upon English standards in language was "extremely prejudicial [to] our political interest in a variety of ways."[5] It was an easy conversion from writing on neutrality to advocating an independent standard of language, and for Webster it represented no diminution of his efforts on behalf of an independent America culturally strong enough to preserve that independence.

[4] November 12, 1807, in Warfel, *Letters of Noah Webster*, p. 295.
[5] *Ibid.*

"... To Dissolve the Charm of Veneration for Foreign Authorities ..."

On the first publication of my *Institutes of the English Language* more than twenty years ago, that eminent classical scholar and divine, the late Dr. Goodrich of Durham, recommended to me to complete a system of elementary principles for the instruction of youth in the English language by compiling and publishing a dictionary. Whatever respect I was inclined to pay to that gentleman's opinion, I could not at that time believe myself qualified for such an undertaking, and various private considerations afterwards interposed to retard its execution. My studies, however, have occasionally had reference to an ultimate accomplishment of such a work, and for a few years past they have been directed immediately to that object. As I have advanced in my investigations, I have been at every step more and more impressed with the importance of this work; and an acquaintance with the Saxon language, the mother tongue of the English, has convinced me that a careful revision of our present dictionaries is absolutely necessary to a correct knowledge of the language.

To men who have been accustomed to repose almost implicit confidence in the authors of our principal dictionaries and grammars, it may appear at first incredible that such writers as Johnson and Lowth should have mistaken many of the fundamental principles of the language. But that such is the fact will appear certain to any man who will read a few pages in a Saxon author.

* * *

Some change of definitions is rendered necessary by new discoveries. Thus, *coral* was formerly supposed to be, and is defined, a marine *plant,* but late inquiries prove it to be an *animal* production. Gold is called in our dictionaries the heaviest of the metals, which description, since the discovery of platina, is become incorrect.

Some words are either new in the United States or, what is more usual, English words have received a new sense. Words of these kinds, when in general use in a state or number of states, or sanctioned by public authority in laws and judicial proceedings, are admitted into this work. When the use is local, that circumstance is noted. Thus the system of taxation in Connecticut has converted *fourfold* into a verb; as have the laws of New York and Pennsylvania, the word *docket;* and the practice of courts in many states, the word *default.* The system of ecclesiastical polity in some states has given a new meaning to *association* and *consociation;* the course of commercial transactions and the system of finance have originated new terms, as *dutiable, customable, irredeemable.* The farmer *girdles* his trees, the planter *gins* his cotton or stocks up the *rattoons* of his sugar cane, altho the language of England furnishes him with no words with meanings suited to his ideas. The merchant imports his *romals, humhums, bastas,* and *gurrahs*—new species of cloths in this country, some perhaps destined to be of durable use, with their foreign names; others, with their names, to slide into disuse and oblivion. *Lots* and *locations* of land, with *located* and *unlocated rights,* form in this country a new language, to which the British people are strangers.

In every country where the English language is used, improvements will continually demand the use of new terms. The artist invents his *telegraph;* the chemist, his *pyrometer* and *gazometer;* and the philosopher discovers *galvanism;* while the physician introduces *vaccination* to restrain the ravages of disease and mitigate the evils of human life. The chemist and mineralogist, by decomposing the materials of the atmosphere and the globe, discover new substances, combinations, and properties which require new names; the navigator explores the distant part of the earth and returns with animals, plants, and marine productions before unknown; while a new system of civil polity in the western world originates new ideas and brings into question the *constitutionality* of powers, *irrepealability* of laws, and the *removability* of men from office.

Thus the English, like every living language, is in a state of progression, as rapid now as at any former period, even more rapid than before the great Dr. Johnson "flattered himself that he might fix the language and put a stop to alterations"—an idea as chimerical as that of Sheridan and Walker, who have attempted to make the mouthing enunciation of the stage a fixed standard of national pronunciation. It is fruitless to attempt to fix that which is in its nature changeable; and to fix which, beyond the power of alteration, would be the greatest evil that could happen to a living language. "If the language of theology," says Johnson, "were extracted from Hooker, and the translation of the bible; the terms of natural knowledge from Bacon; the phrases of policy, war, and navigation from Raleigh; the dialect of poetry and fiction from Spenser and Sidney; and the diction of common life from Shakespear, few ideas would be lost to mankind for want of English words in which they might be expressed." How short sighted was that learned man! Many words found in all the authors mentioned are no longer used, and two of those writers cannot be read without a glossary. Scarcely was this lexicographer in his grave when new discoveries in natural history originated a language almost entirely new in some of its branches and changed the whole face of the science. From the changes in civil policy, manners, arts of life, and other circumstances attending the settlement of English colonies in America, most of the language of heraldry, hawking, hunting, and especially that of the old feudal and hierarchal establishments of England will become utterly extinct in this country; much of it already forms a part of the neglected rubbish of antiquity.

The Hebrew, Greek, and Latin languages, with the Teutonic and all its branches—the German, Dutch, Swiss, Swedish, Danish, English, and Icelandic—proceeded from one parent stock, the identity of their origin being discoverable in the radicals of many words common to them all. The English as a main branch of that stock now becomes the parent stock of the languages of the countries colonized by British subjects. The descendants of the settlers in the Indies, in America, in New Holland, in the South Seas will continue forever to speak the English language, but with numerous variations arising from difference of climate, plants, animals, arts, manufactures, manners, and policy.

In each of the countries peopled by Englishmen a distinct dialect of the language will gradually be formed, the principal of which will be that of the United States. In fifty years from this time the *American-English* will be spoken by more people than all the other dialects of the language, and in one hundred and thirty years by more people than any other language on the globe, not excepting the Chinese. Those words which express ideas common to the several nations will remain so nearly the same in all the dialects as to render mutual intercourse easy, a circumstance for which the citizens of each country will be much indebted to the art of printing, which will retard the progress of variations. But those terms in Great Britain which express local ideas only will be lost in the dialects of India and America, while local circumstances among the descendants of the English in their new settlements will originate new words or give to old words new significations which will never be generally received or known in Great Britain.

With these extensive views of this subject have I entered upon the plan of compiling for my fellow citizens a dictionary which shall exhibit a far more correct state of the language than any work of this kind. In the meantime, this compend is offered to the public as a convenient manual. No person acquainted with the difficulties attending such a compilation will flatter himself or the public that any thing like perfection is within the compass of one man's abilities. Nothing like this is here promised. All that I have attempted, and all that I can believe to be executed, is a dictionary with considerable improvements, a work required by the advanced and advancing state of science and arts. The dictionaries of a living language must be revised every half century or must necessarily be erroneous and imperfect.

I am not unapprized of the objections which have been made to this design, even by good men and sincere patriots. But it will readily occur to a candid mind that a person who has never turned his attention to this subject may entertain views of it very different from those of a man who has directed his investigations to it for some years and, not satisfied with modern criticisms, has mounted to higher sources of knowledge. Candid men, however, will not differ much on the subject when they have the advantage of the same evidence; and that the great body of my fellow citizens are of this character is beyond a question.

From a different class of men, if such are to be found, whose criticisms would sink the literature of this country even lower than the distorted representations of foreign reviewers, whose veneration for trans-Atlantic authors leads them to hold American writers in unmerited contempt—from such men I neither expect nor solicit favor. Men who take pains to find and to exhibit to the world proofs of our national inferiority in talents and acquirements are certainly not destined to decide the ultimate fate of this performance.

However arduous the task, and however feeble my powers of body and mind, a thorough conviction of the necessity and importance of the undertaking has overcome my fears and objections and determined me to make one effort to dissolve the charm of veneration for foreign authorities which fascinates the mind of men in this country and holds them in the chains of illusion. In the investigation of this subject great labor is to be sustained and numerous difficulties encountered; but with a humble dependence on Divine favor for the preservation of my life and health, I shall prosecute the work with diligence and execute it with a fidelity suited to its importance.

"The Young Hercules of Genius in America Chained to His Cradle"

From *A Letter to the Honorable John Pickering,* 1816

EDITOR'S COMMENTS

So significant an undertaking as Webster's dictionary could not help but arouse considerable criticism, especially in the charged atmosphere of the early nineteenth century. To challenge the authority of the great Dr. Johnson and other standards of English style was to test any man's daring; to undertake it in the face of established hostility to one's efforts required confidence bordering on temerity. Indeed, *An American Dictionary of the English Language* was completed in spite of a welter of criticism, both veiled and direct, to all of which Webster was acutely sensitive. Some criticisms he chose to disregard, especially as he grew more confident of the validity of his objective; others so touched his pride and aroused his indignation that he could not resist a rebuttal. Throughout his life Webster held to his youthful creed that "the criticisms of those who know more will be received with gratitude; the censure or ridicule of those who know less will be inexcusable." (See Selection One, p. 23.) In the infighting of literary controversy, as in his earlier career as a publicist, Webster proved himself an effective combatant. Some of his most arresting prose was written in retaliation for what he considered unjust criticism.

In the year 1817 Webster was sufficiently aroused by the criticism of one of those "whose veneration for trans-Atlantic authors leads them to hold American writers in unmerited contempt" (see Selection Nine, p. 136) that he prepared a pamphlet of more than fifty pages in reply. The instigator was John Pickering of Boston, who, in an effort to extinguish the notion that Americans had created valid new words, had presented a paper to the American Academy of Science entitled *A Vocabulary or Collection of Words and Phrases which have been supposed to be peculiar to the United States.* To it Pickering prefixed a

Memoir on the Present State of the English Language in the United States in which he attacked those "ridiculous novelties" perpetrated by "conceited individuals" that brought down upon American letters the scorn and contempt of "well-educated Englishmen." Excerpts from Webster's lengthy and detailed reply, entitled *A Letter to the Honorable John Pickering,* comprise the accompanying selection.

Expressing with force his own spirit of independence and his contempt for those who looked to England for their standards of taste and style in literature, Webster demonstrates here, with unusual vigor, his willingness to "measure swords" in defense of his objectives. His letter also indicates that he saw himself in combat with a real, not an imaginary, enemy in the lingering cultural dependence upon Great Britain. Webster's reply, though poorly organized, shows some of the fruits of his linguistic research and, consequently, greater confidence and sophistication than was evident in his earlier essays on language.

"The Young Hercules of Genius in America Chained to His Cradle"

New words should not be introduced into a copious language without reason, nor contrary to its analogies. But a living language must keep pace with improvements in knowledge and with the multiplication of ideas. Those who would entirely restrain the practice of using new words seem not to consider that the limit they *now* prescribe would have been as just and rational a thousand or two thousand years ago as it is at this period. If it should be said we have words enough to express all our ideas, it may be truly answered, so had our ancestors when they left the plains of Germany, or when they first crossed the Hellespont, or when they left the soil of Persia. And what then? Would the words they then used be now sufficient for *our* purpose? And who can define the bounds of future improvement? Who will venture to alledge that men have not yet as much to learn as they have already learnt? The smallest acquaintance with the history of human society and improvement ought to silence the critics on this subject.

Nor are we to believe that two nations inhabiting countries separated by a wide ocean can preserve a perfect uniformity of language. If a perfect uniformity cannot be produced or preserved in two distant counties in England, how is this object to be effected between the English in Great Britain and their descendants in America, India, or New Holland? Let history answer the question. The art of printing, interchange of books, and commercial intercourse will retard the progress of mutation and diversities, but no human means can prevent some changes and the adaptation of language to diversities of condition and improvement. The process of a living language is like the motion of a broad river which flows with a slow, silent, *irresistible* current.

The preceding remarks will enable us to decide on the heavy charge of introducing *barbarisms* and *barbarous phraseology* into the language, so often alledged against American writers by our English brethren. Harsh names, derision, and contempt are coarse and cheap commodities, the stock of the hucksters in literature who cannot deal in more valuable wares. In the truck and barter of such commodities let us have no concern.

A *barbarism* in language is strictly a foreign word. In this literal sense the English would hardly admit the application of the word, for it would include *burlesque, grotesque, groupe, pique,* and many others which their best authors use without hesitation. I know of no sense in which the word barbarous can be justly applied to words, except that words are of foreign origin, or not formed from any legitimate root, or formed in a manner not warranted by any rule of analogy. So far as words deviate from established analogies they violate the correctness and purity of the language. A new derivative or compound word formed according to our idiomatic rules on legitimate roots is *not a barbarism.* The extension of the sense of a word to *new,* but *analogous,* ideas is *not a barbarism*—half the significations of our words are of this kind. *Old words* are *not barbarisms* merely because they are old or going into disuse. Examine the subject by these principles and name, if you please, the *American* barbarisms.

*   *   *

I could extend these remarks by multiplying examples and prove by numerous facts that the English themselves are chargeable with most of the anomalies and barbarisms in our language. In a multitude of instances, wherever in orthography the alternative has been presented of a regular and an anomalous spelling, they have chosen that which is anomalous. Thus *leather* is generally written in our mother tongue *lether*, rarely *leather;* but they have adopted the latter. I must not, however, pursue this subject.

You have suggested, Sir, in your Preface, that "in this country, as in England, we have thirsty reformers and presumptuous sciolists who would unsettle the whole of our admirable language for the purpose of making it conform to their whimsical notions of propriety." This is a heavy accusation, Sir, from a gentleman of your talents, liberality, and candor. Sciolists we may have in multitudes, but who are the men who would *unsettle* the *whole of our language?* Can you name the men, or any of them, either in this country or in England? Surely the finger of scorn ought to be pointed at the men who are base enough to wish, and sottish enough to attempt, to unsettle a whole language. I am confident, Sir, that deliberate reflection will induce you to retract a charge so injurious to your fellow citizens. It certainly becomes you, and the character you maintain in society, to learn the distinction between an attempt to find what the language is and an attempt to unsettle its principles. Whether you number me with the thirsty reformers and presumptuous sciolists is a fact which I shall take no pains to discover, nor, if known, would the fact give me the smallest concern. My studies have been sometimes directed to philology for the exclusive purpose of ascertaining and unfolding its principles, correcting abuses, and supplying the defect of rules in our elementary treatises. In the course of my researches I have discovered a multitude of errors and false principles and numerous defects in such treatises; and as I have pushed my inquiries probably much farther than any other man, I am satisfied that the evidence I can lay before the public will convince you that there is a rich mine of knowledge to be opened on this subject that your English friends have never yet discovered.

*   *   *

The truth is, the grammar of our language is in a very imperfect state—full of error and confusion. To disembarrass it from this confusion is a work of no small labor and requiring the profoundest knowledge of its origin and real structure. Lindley Murray, a man of real worth indeed, but possessing less talents and erudition than many of his predecessors, has left the subject in nearly as imperfect a state as he found it.

I have attempted to elucidate some of its principles and have found it necessary to deviate in some particulars from systems heretofore received, and for this reason have been censured. When a man proposes any thing contrary to established opinions, the question asked is, "Have any of the rulers believed on him?" If not, reject his doctrines as those of a presumptuous sciolist. But I will not conform to a practice in morals or to a principle in science when I have full evidence or certain knowledge that it is wrong. Men may fill their books with citations from Lowth and Johnson, Harris and Blair and Campbell, and reviewers without number; but if I know from better authorities that their opinions are erroneous, I shall submit to any harsh treatment and hard names rather than secure popularity by falling into the common current of error. When Lowth and Johnson, for example, call *if* a conjunction and I discover that it is a verb with no connective use any more than *go* or *come,* I will not call it a conjunction. When Horne Tooke says that *for* is from a word signifying *cause, motive,* that *from* signifies *beginning,* and *to* signifies *act, effect,* and I find, by resorting to higher sources, that this is a mistake, I shall differ from the author, whatever risk I may encounter; nor shall I believe with him that *truth* is what a man thinks or *trows* when I know that this opinion is not *true.*

Great as I believe the intellectual powers of Johnson to have been, I cannot place implicit confidence in a man who informs us he does not well understand the words *staddle* and *stud,* nor the meaning of *warp* in one of the finest passages of Milton. Nor can I submit my opinion to the decisions of the writers on rhetoric (Blair and Campbell, if I do not misremember) who tell us the Latin language has no articles and boast of the superiority of the English in this respect.

*   *   *

This shows how much writers and learners are misled by names and distinctions—repeating them like parrots, age after age, without any correct ideas of the reasons on which they are built or knowing whether they are founded on reasons or not. Had the English compilers of grammars been guided by principles instead of the authority of custom, they would have perceived that if there is any use in making the article a distinct part of speech, *this* and *that* should be joined with *the;* for if there is a difference, it is in favor of *this* and *that,* which mark the definiteness of nouns with more exactness than *the.* In our mother tongue they are called articles. But the truth is, there is neither necessity nor propriety in the distinction—the words called *articles* (an insignificant term) are adjectives, expressing something that belongs to nouns; as *number,* like *an, unus; sex,* as the Spanish and Italian *lo, la,* and the Latin *ille, illa, hic, haec;* or limitation, as in English *the, this, that, these, those, &c.* It is the same with the Greek article.

* * *

You form a supposition that the time may arrive when Americans shall no longer be able to understand the works of Milton, Pope, Swift, and Addison without the aid of a *translation,* which would certainly be a great misfortune. Were it not for my personal respect for you, I might oppose to this supposition another which is nearly as probable, that the rivers in America will turn their courses and flow from the sea to the tops of the hills.

But, Sir, if such an event should take place, the people of this country must learn *English* and read the English authors as we do Livy and Caesar. One thing is very certain: the works of Milton, Pope, and Addison will be read by Americans till our descendants divest themselves of their leading-strings, grow up to manhood in intellectual vigor, and write books that they like better. And it may be proved by European authorities that this event is either impossible or very remote—so remote that you and I, Sir, can have very little interest in the event.

You take some pains to ascertain the point whether the people of this country now speak and write the English language with purity. The result is that we have, in several instances, departed from the standard of the language as spoken and written in England at the present day. Be it so. It is equally true that the English have departed from the standard as it appears in the works of Addison. And this is acknowledged by yourself (page 22). It is equally true that Addison, Pope, and Johnson deviated from the standard of the age of Elizabeth. And now, Sir, where is the remedy?

Let me remark, Sir, that writers on this subject, both in Great Britain and America, seem to assume as a fact that the language has arrived to its *ne plus* of perfection—that it is incapable of improvement and that it is our duty to limit its progress. On no other hypothesis can an attempt to fix it in its present state be vindicated. On this subject I have already expressed my opinion—that a language must keep pace with improvements in knowledge, and that no definable limtis can be assigned to a living language because such limits cannot be assigned to future discoveries and advances in science. To arrest the progress of a language is therefore impossible—and, if possible, would be a misfortune. A similar opinion seems to have been entertained by Dr. Johnson, that certain writers whom he mentions might furnish all the words the English nation would ever want. What would that great man have said had he lived to see the improvements since made in the various branches of natural history—in chemistry, botany, geology, and mineralogy?

You maintain that Englishmen are competent judges of the changes of language in this country. Not better judges, Sir, than Americans are of their own deviations from English practice, or of the changes in Great Britain. I can furnish as long a catalogue of the changes introduced in England as any Englishman can of *our* deviations. Let me add, Sir, that when national prejudices are buried in the grave with those who entertain them, many specimens of style already produced in this country will stand as high in the estimation of impartial judges as the best English productions. The vindication of Judge Chase is as fine a composition as ever issued from a British press.

With regard to the British reviewers, whose opinions you have cited at some length, I would briefly remark that they stand much higher in your estimation than in mine. Some of the reviews are conducted by able men, but these are all subject to like passions— their views of the subject under consideration are extremely

limited. Not one of them, as far as I can learn, ever attempts to
find a rule of decision except in their own practice. Whatever
agrees with that is right; whatever differs is wrong. And, what is
singular, no writers have introduced as many new words as reviewers; and almost every new word found in American writings,
as your own book proves, has a precedent in some British review. I
blame not the use of the new words if occasion requires them, but I
must censure the critic that charges them to an innovating spirit in
my countrymen.

The reviewers are perpetually writing about a *standard of
language*—a thing, in its own nature, impossible. In every nation
there are certain authors whose writings stand higher in public
estimation than those of others, but not one of them is faultless;
and even when they are correct the critics will sometimes condemn
them, which proves that the best writers will not *fix a standard*.
Thus the modern pamphleteers are prating about the style and
language of Addison, Dryden, Pope, and Swift as THE STANDARD of
good English; but look into Lowth's grammar and there you will
see a multitude of words in those authors condemned as ungram-
matical. Some of them are wrong in principle; many of them are
right in principle, but *wrong* according to modern usage, or wrong
only in the opinion of critics. Thus Lowth condemns in Addison
the use of *was* in the second person—"knowing that *you was* my
old master's good friend"—and the like use of it in Bolingbroke
and Pope. But these authors wrote genuine English, and the criticisms upon this and many other words and phrases used in Addison's age are proofs of the low state of philological knowledge,
which reproaches the erudition of the present day. *You was, we
was, they was* are not vulgar corruptions, they are genuine English
in the Gothic dialect, which is now used by nine tenths of the
people. Our Saxon books are mostly written in the dialect of the
Anglo-Saxons, and on this dialect our grammar rules are chiefly
constructed. It is strange, however, that the obvious fact, this
common and almost universal use of the Gothic dialect of the
substantive verb, should have passed unnoticed. We use three or

four distinct roots in our substantive verb: *am; are, art, were; is, was;* and *be.*

* * *

Addison and Pope wrote according to the prevailing custom of the nation, and all the rules and censures of the compilers of grammars cannot banish the customary use of this old and established dialect. It is idle to attempt it—the Greek writers and critics had more good sense than to censure the use of the different dialects in *their* language. The use of them in Homer has ever been considered a beauty.

You admit that the language of the United States has *changed less than might have been expected* considering the time which has elapsed since our ancestors emigrated. Why less than could have been expected? If changes are to be expected at all, the expectation must rest upon a knowledge of some *causes of change* that are beyond control—and this is a concession which overthrows all your reasoning against such changes. This is the real fact, Sir. Let it be observed, by the way, that so far as a difference between the language of Englishmen and of Americans consists in our use of words obsolete in the higher circles in Great Britain, the change is not in *our* practice but in that of Englishmen. The fault, if any, is *theirs.* When they declaim with vehemence against *innovations,* let them not censure our adherence to old words and phrases, manifesting a disposition *not* to innovate.

You tell us that, as a general rule, we should *undoubtedly* avoid all those words which are noticed by English authors of reputation as expressions with which *they are unacquainted.* As a lawyer, Sir, you may easily make several points in this case.

First—How shall it be satisfactorily ascertained who are *authors of reputation?* With regard to some writers we should tolerably well agree, but in regard to reviewers, who are the men that *notice words,* we doubtless should differ very widely even if we knew the men; but a great difficulty is we do not know who they are.

Second—How shall we know, when we are writing or speaking, whether Englishmen are acquainted with this or that particular word which we wish to use? Shall we send across the Atlantic to ascertain? And to whom shall we send?

Thirdly—We are embarrassed with another difficulty—some Englishmen may be acquainted with words of which others are totally ignorant; and how shall we discover the extent of every reputable author's knowledge? We may gain a partial knowledge from reviews, but many people here have occasion to write who do not see British reviews.

With regards to *corruptions* which, you remark, are gradually insinuating themselves into our language, it is proved, I trust, in the preceding observations, that the alarm on this subject is unfounded. The use of old legitimate words cannot be called a *corruption;* the affixing of new significations to old words is usually the necessary result of a new state of society and government or of an intercourse with new objects, or it proceeds from the regular principles of analogy in the formation and application of words which have been established from the beginning of the world.

Mr. [Charles James] Fox, it is said, would not admit a word into his history for which he had not the authority of Dryden. I hope, Sir, he would not admit *every* word that Dryden has authorized. *Miscorrect,* in his life of Virgil, is a *new* word, Sir, and perhaps a very good one, but the use of it falls under the same charge of innovation which is now so liberally bestowed on Americans. But *critic* for *criticise, comment* as a verb transitive, and *dispose* as a noun I believe Mr. Fox would not use, even upon the authority of Dryden. But, Sir, please attend to Dryden's own opinions on this subject, expressed in his dedication to the Earl of Mulgrave: "If sounding words are not of our own growth and manufacture, who shall hinder me to import them from a foreign country? I carry not out the treasure of the nation, which is never to return; but what I bring from Italy, I spend in England. Here it remains— here it circulates—for if the coin be good, it will pass from one hand to another. I trade both with the living and the dead for the enrichment of our native language. We have enough in England to supply our necessity, but if we will have things of magnificence and splendor, we must get them by commerce. Poetry requires ornament, and that is not to be had from our old Teuton monosyllables; therefore if I find any elegant word in a classic author, I propose it to be naturalized by using it myself; and if the public approves of it, the bill passes."

This is the language of Dryden—and the principles here stated have influenced other distinquished writers to enrich our language with words borrowed from Greece, Rome, France, and Spain. The like principles will continue to enrich it, I trust, in spite of the narrow views and illiberal criticisms of reviewers.

You frequently mention in the course of your observations that a word is not in the dictionaries, as a kind of silent reproof for the use of it. Pray, Sir, in what British dictionary except Entick's do you find the word *statement!* In what British dictionary do you find *expenditure, classification, informality, simplify, admissibility, combinable, diplomatic, sanction* a verb; *insubordination, indorsor, indorsee, payor, payee, substantiate,* &c., except one or two of them in Mason's supplement to Johnson? Surely, Sir, you would not denounce these and similar words as not authorized English words because they are not in dictionaries.

You also frequently mention the insertion of words in the new edition of Johnson by the Reverend Mr. Todd. Of this edition I have seen but one number, and from that I judge that the editor will improve the vocabulary. But his practice of assigning reasons for his insertion of words appears to be an improper compliance with the hyper-critical spirit of the age and an evidence of too little confidence in his own judgement and qualifications for the task he has undertaken. It will serve only to involve the public in perplexity. In regard to the etymology of words which he attempts to elucidate, I perceive that he has undertaken what he does not fully understand, and if he executes this part of the work as he has begun it, he will do more harm than good.

With regard to the general principle that we must use only such words as the English use, let me repeat that the restricton is, in the nature of the thing, impracticable, and the demand that we should observe it is as improper as it is arrogant. Equally impertinent is it to ridicule us for retaining the use of genuine English words because they happen to be obsolete in London or in the higher circles of life. There are many instances in which we retain the genuine use of words and the genuine English pronunciation, which they have corrupted; in pronunciation they have introduced more corruptions within half a century than were ever before introduced in five centuries, not even excepting the periods of conquest. Many of these changes in England are attributable to false principles introduced into popular elementary books written by mere sciolists in language and diffused by the instrumentality of the stage—that prolific parent of corruption. Let the English remove the beam from their own eye before they attempt to pull the mote from ours; and before they laugh at our vulgar *keow, geown, neow,* let them discard their polite *keind* and *geuide*—a fault precisely similar in origin and equally a perversion of genuine English pronunciation.

I left college with the same veneration for English writers and the same confidence in their opinions which most of my countrymen now possess, and I adopted their errors without examination. After many years of research I am compelled to withdraw much of that confidence and to look with astonishment upon the errors and false principles which they have propagated, some of them of far more consequence than any which have been mentioned in the preceding remarks. I wish to be on good terms with the English— it is my interest and the interest of my fellow citizens to treat them as friends and brethren. But I will be neither frowned, nor ridiculed, into error and a servile imitation of practices which I know or believe to be corrupt. I will examine subjects for myself and endeavor to find the truth and to defend it, whether it accords with English opinions or not. If I must measure swords with their travellers and their reviewers on the subject under consideration, I shall not decline the combat. There is nothing which, in my opinion, so debases the genius and the character of my countrymen as the implicit confidence they place in English authors and their unhesitating submission to their *opinions,* their *derision,* and their *frowns.* But I trust the time will come when the English will be convinced that the intellectual faculties of their descendants have not degenerated in America, and that we can contend with them in LETTERS with as much success as upon the OCEAN.

I am not ignorant, Sir, of the narrowness of the sphere which I now occupy. Secluded in a great measure from the world, with small means and no adventitious aids from men of science, with little patronage to extend my influence and powerful enmities to circumscribe it, what can my efforts avail in attempting to counteract a current of opinion? Yet I am not accustomed to despondence. I have contributed in a small degree to the instruction of at least four millions of the rising generation; and it is not unreasonable to expect that a few seeds of improvement, planted by my hand, may germinate and grow and ripen into valuable fruit when my remains shall be mingled with the dust.

"... True Dignity of Character"

From *Letters to a Young Gentleman Commencing His Education*, 1823

EDITOR'S COMMENTS

Of Noah Webster's conversion to Congregationalism in 1808 it has been said, "At fifty he made up his mind and never changed it again."[1] It is true that approximately from that date the pattern of Webster's life falls into settled contrast with the varied and often hectic career he had carried on until that time. Where excited interest in national affairs had once held sway, a preoccupation with morality and piety now dominated, and vigorous radicalism abdicated in favor of a perhaps more natural heritage, that of "Steady Habit" Federalism.

Webster's withdrawal, for economic reasons, to Amherst, Massachusetts, in 1812 was not, however, a denial of his past. Still energetic and civic-minded, he was active in the affairs of both church and state, serving in the Massachusetts legislature and as a manager of the First Church, helping to found Amherst College, and playing an important role in the inception of the Hartford Convention. He did some farming, but labored chiefly on his great dictionary. His faith in the tradition of steady habits kept him at the laborious task of completing his awesome undertaking now that he had lost his enthusiasm for political affairs, which had been the focal point for the development of his principles of cultural independence.

In 1822 Webster wrote his daughter, "We pass life as usual. We retire to rest at the usual hour; rise in the morning, eat when we are hungry and sometimes when we are not. I write; your mother patches and darns."[2] It was a quiet and rewarding existence, one in which the aging Webster had time for reflection as well as work. Here Webster

[1] Warfel, *Noah Webster: Schoolmaster to America*, p. 353.
[2] Warfel, *Letters of Noah Webster*, pp. 408–9.

154

settled many of his final attitudes toward life and, in patriarchal fashion, dispensed them to others.

In 1823, just prior to his trip to Europe and England to complete his research for the dictionary and shortly after his final move back to New Haven, Webster published a volume entitled *Letters to a Young Gentleman Commencing His Education: To which is subjoined a brief History of the United States*. The observations on manners and morals that constitute Letter I of the volume (and the accompanying selection) are the settled views of Webster's conservative old age. The emphasis upon religion as the foundation of morality, the ingrained notion that property is the wellspring of responsible government, distaste for the entertainment arts, and downright distrust of active politics delineate the almost classic conservatism into which the sixty-five-year-old patriarch had settled. Significantly directed at the youth of America, this sober advice, in presenting the distilled wisdom of one New England Federalist, speaks for a generation.

"... True Dignity of Character"

My Dear Friend,

As you are now commencing a course of classical education and need the guidance of those who have preceded you in the same course, you cannot but receive with kindness and treat with attention the remarks of a friend whose affection for you excites in him a deep solicitude for your future reputation and happiness. I feel the more desirous to furnish you with some hints for the direction of your studies, for I have experienced the want of such helps myself, no small portion of my life having been spent in correcting the errors of my early education.

It has been often remarked that men are the creatures of habit. The rudiments of knowledge we receive by tradition, and our first actions are, in a good degree, modelled by imitation. Nor ought it to be otherwise. The respect which young persons feel for their parents, superiors, and predecessors is not less the dictate of reason than the requirement of heaven; and the propensity to imitation is no less natural than it may be useful. These principles, however, like many others, when pursued or indulged to an extreme, produce evil effects, as they often lead the young to embrace error as well as truth. Some degree of confidence in the opinions of those whom we respect is always a duty—in the first stages of life our confidence in parents must be implicit, and our obedience to their will, complete and unreserved. In later stages of life, as the intellectual faculties expand and the reasoning power gains strength, implicit confidence in the opinions even of the most distinguished men ceases to be a duty. We are to regard their opinions only as *probably* correct, but refer the ultimate decision of this point to evidence to be collected from our own reasonings or researches. All men are liable to err, and a knowledge of this fact should excite in us constant solicitude to obtain satisfactory reasons for every opinion we embrace.

As men are furnished with powers of reason, it is obviously the design of the creator that reason should be employed as their guide in every stage of life. But reason without cultivation, without experience, and without the aids of revelation, is a miserable guide; it often errs from ignorance and more often from the impulse of passion. The first questions a rational being should ask himself are *Who made me? Why was I made? What is my duty?* The proper answers to these questions, and the practical results, constitute, my dear friend, the whole business of life.

Now, reason, unaided by revelation, cannot answer these questions. The experience of the pagan world has long since determined this point. Revelation alone furnishes satisfactory information on these subjects. Let it then be the first study that occupies your mind to learn from the Scriptures the character and will of your maker, the end or purpose for which he gave you being and intellectual powers, and the duties he requires you to perform. In all that regards faith and practice, the Scriptures furnish the principles, precepts, and rules by which you are to be guided. Your reputation among men, your own tranquillity of mind in this life, and all rational hope of future happiness depend on an exact conformity of conduct to the commands of God revealed in the sacred oracles.

The duties of men are summarily comprised in the Ten Commandments, consisting of two tables: one comprehending the duties which we owe immediately to God; the other, the duties we owe to our fellow men. Christ himself has reduced these commandments under two general precepts, which enjoin upon us to love the Lord our God with all our heart, with all our soul, with all our mind, and with all our strength, and to love our neighbor as ourselves. On these two commandments hang all the law and the prophets—that is, they comprehend the substance of all the doctrines and precepts of the Bible, or the whole of religion.[3]

*   *   *

In selecting books for reading, be careful to choose such as furnish the best helps to improvement in morals, literature, arts, and science, preferring profit to pleasure and instruction to amusement. A small portion of time may be devoted to such reading as tends to relax the mind, and to such bodily amusements as serve to invigorate muscular strength and the vital functions. But the greatest part of life is to be employed in useful labors and in various indispensable duties—private, social, and public. Man has but little time to spare for the gratification of the senses and the imagination. I would therefore caution you against the fascinations of plays, novels, romances, and that species of descriptive writing which is employed to embellish common objects without much enlarging the bounds of knowledge or to paint imaginary scenes which only excite curiosity and a temporary interest and then vanish in empty air.

The readers of books may be comprehended in two classes— those who read chiefly for amusement and those who read for instruction. The first, and far the most numerous class, give their money and their time for private gratification; the second employ both for the acquisition of knowledge which they expect to apply to some useful purpose. The first gain subjects of conversation and social entertainment; the second acquire the means of public usefulness and of private elevation of character. The readers of the first class are so numerous, and the thirst for novelty so insatiable, that the country must be deluged with tales and fiction; and if you suffer yourself to be hurried along with the current of popular feeling, not only your *time*, but your *mind*, will be dissipated; your native faculties, instead of growing into masculine vigor, will languish into imbecility. Bacon and Newton did not read tales and

[3] A discussion of the several Commandments has been omitted here.—Ed.

novels; their great minds were nourished with very different aliment.

Theatrical entertainments have strong attractions, especially for the young and the thoughtless. They are vindicated as a rational and instructive amusement, and men of sober judgement and sound morals sometimes attend them—not, however, I believe, with the expectation of gaining useful knowledge, but for the purpose of being entertained with seeing the powers of the actors. They are pleased to see one man imitate another, and the more exact the imitation, the more are they delighted. The representation of elevated characters has a show of dignity; the low scenes are mere vulgar buffoonery. Very few plays, however, are free from sentiments which are offensive to moral purity. Many of them abound with ribaldry and vulgarity too gross for exhibition before persons of delicacy and refined manners. Before I can believe the stage to be a school of virtue, I must demand proof that a single profligate has ever been reformed or a single man or woman made a Christian by its influence. And let me ask what sort of entertainment is that in which a thin partition only separates the nobleman from his lackey and the duchess from her kitchen-maid, in which the gentleman and the lady associate at the same board with the footman, the oysterman, and the woman of the town, and all partake of the same fare! With what sentiments must superior beings look down on this motley school of morality?

In forming your connections in society, be careful to select for your companions young men of good breeding and of virtuous principles and habits. The company of the profligate and irreligious is to be shunned as poison. You cannot always avoid some intercourse with men of dissolute lives, but you can always select for your intimate associates men of good principles and unimpeachable character. Never maintain a familiar intercourse with the profane, the lewd, the intemperate, the gamester, or the scoffer at religion. Towards men of such character the common civilities of life are to be observed; beyond these, nothing is required of men who reverence the divine precepts and who desire to "keep themselves unspotted from the world."

I would advise you never to become a member of any association the object of which is concealed. If times and circumstances, in any country and at any period of the world, have rendered such associations necessary for the protection of person or property or for the reformation of public abuses no longer tolerable, such circumstances do not exist in this country. Secret societies or clubs may have innocent and even good objects in view; but concealment always exposes them to suspicion, and it seems incompatible with true dignity of character to expose one's self voluntarily to such suspicions. A good man—a man of truly philanthropic principles—will always direct his views to valuable objects of public or private utility, and these require no secrecy. Associations for intellectual improvement, for executing useful undertakings, and for combining and giving effect to exertions of benevolence are highly laudable. But always bear in mind this important fact, that men are all members of one great family, and benevolence should know no bounds but the limits of this family. It should therefore be our aim not to attempt to narrow the limits of benevolence which God himself has prescribed. It may well be questioned whether, as society is now constituted, the partialities of men, originating in distinctions, national and local, political and religious, do not contract the benevolent principles of our nature within much narrower limits than is consistent with Christian morality. No philanthropist can see, without pain, nations and states, parties and religious sects, perpetually struggling to secure, each to itself, some exclusive or superior advantages in property, power, or influence, and often by means base and dishonorable. This conduct usually originates in pride or selfish views, as unfriendly to social happiness as they are repugnant to the will of our common father. Whether in politics or religion, this is an odious trait in the human character.

When we consider that men are all brethren of the same family, all created with similar capacities and vested with the same natural rights, and in this country all enjoying equal civil and religious rights under the protection of law, all equally entitled to security and public privileges, all placed under the same moral discipline, and all destined to the same end—how disgusting is it to see one

party or one sect arrogating to itself superior merit or proud distinction and saying to others, *"Stand by thyself—come not near me,
for I am holier than thou!"* Yet such is the language of parties—
often in religion, always in government. When the fundamental
principles of government or our holy religion are assaulted, good
men must unite to defend them. But the most numerous and most
violent parties that trouble society spring from private ambition
and interest, when no principles are in jeopardy, or from an undue
attachment to speculative opinions in politics, or to the externals of
religion; and in such parties the human character is displayed in all
its depravity and degradation. In the tranquil condition of affairs in
this country, when our citizens enjoy all the privileges which good
men can desire and more than many can enjoy without abuse, a
disposition to exalt one class of citizens and to depress another is a
foul reproach to men—a fouler reproach to Christians.

Never, my dear friend, degrade yourself by an unhallowed
alliance with a political party that assumes the right of controlling
all public affairs, to the exclusion of other citizens who have equal
rights and equal property to defend, and equal claims to a share in
the management of that property. The attempts, and often successful attempts, in this country to exclude one class of citizens from
any control in legislation over the property which their industry
has acquired and which bears its proportion of the burdens of
government is as rude an assault on liberty as ever disgraced the
annals of despotism. Accustom yourself from your youth to consider all men as your brethren, and know no distinction between
fellow citizens except that which they make themselves by their
virtues or their *vices*, by their *worth* or their *meanness*.

A republican form of government is evidently the most rational
form that men have devised for the protection of person and
property and for securing liberty. But hitherto no means have been
devised to guard this form of government from abuse and corruption. Men in republics are as wicked and as selfish as in monarchies,
and with far more power to introduce disorders, both into legislation and into the administration of the laws. In republics the
influence of selfish and ambitious men over the weak, the ignorant,

and unsuspecting has its full range of operation, and sooner or later this influence will place in office incompetent men or men who will sacrifice principle to personal emolument or aggrandizement. The corruption of the electors is the first step towards the ruin of republics; and when the sources of power are corrupted, the evil hardly admits of a remedy.

It seems to be a political axiom that republics should be founded on an equality of rights or so constructed as to preserve that equality. But with all the declamation which is heard on this subject, this equality of rights seems not to be understood; the very terms want definition. That all men have an equal right to the protection of their persons, their reputation, and their property is undeniable. But, it may be asked, has a man who has no property to defend, and none to support the expenses of government, an *equal right* to legislate upon property as a man who has property to guard and to apply to the support and defense of his country? May it not be true in a republic that a *majority* of the citizens may possess a *minority* of the property, and may it not happen that the *minor* interests may govern the *major interest?* And in this case, what becomes of the *equality of rights* on which we profess to found a republican government? When the sober, industrious citizen who, by his toil and economy, collects a moderate estate, brings up a family in good habits, and pays his taxes to government finds that his property and virtue give him no influence or advantage as a member of the government over the idle pennyless lounger who earns little and spends that little in vice, paying nothing to government, what attachment can this good citizen feel to the government? What confidence can he place in its administration? What expectation can he entertain of its durability? And what sort of government is that in which the *owners* of the country do not govern it?

Melancholy as this view of the subject is, you are the subject and the citizen of a republic, and in these characters duties will devolve on you of no ordinary magnitude. As a *subject,* yield an entire obedience to the laws and established institutions of society. Never for the paltry consideration of interest resort to deception, concealment, or equivocation to evade your proper share in the burdens of government. As a *citizen*, exercise your rights with integrity and unshaken independence of mind. An obsequious elector who temporizes with party and yields to every varying breeze of popular opinion is a most contemptible character.

In selecting men for office, let principle be your guide. Regard not the particular sect or denomination of the candidate—look to his character as a man of known principle, of tried integrity, and undoubted ability for the office.

It is alleged by men of loose principles, or defective views of the subject, that religion and morality are not necessary or important qualifications for political stations. But the Scriptures teach a different doctrine. They direct that rulers should be men *who rule in the fear of God, able men such as fear God, men of truth hating covetousness.* But if we had no divine instruction on the subject, our own interest would demand of us a strict observance of the principle of these injunctions. And it is to the neglect of this rule of conduct in our citizens that we must ascribe the multiplied frauds, breaches of trust, peculations, and embezzlements of public property which astonish even ourselves, which tarnish the character of our country, which disgrace a republican government, and which will tend to reconcile men to monarchy in other countries and even in our own.

When a citizen gives his suffrage to a man of known immorality, he abuses his trust; he sacrifices not only his own interest but that of his neighbor; he betrays the interest of his country. Nor is it of slight importance that men elected to office should be *able* men— men of talents equal to their stations; men of mature age, experience, and judgement; men of firmness and impartiality. This is particularly true with regard to men who constitute tribunals of justice—the main bulwark of our rights, the citadel that maintains the last struggle of freedom against the inroads of corruption and tyranny. In this citadel should be stationed no raw, inexperienced soldier, no weak, temporizing defender who will obsequiously bend to power or parley with corruption.

One of the surest tests of a man's real worth is the esteem and confidence of those who have long known him and his conduct in domestic and social life. It may be held as generally true that respect spontaneously attaches itself to real worth, and the man of respectable virtues never has occasion to run after respect. Whenever a man is known to seek promotion by intrigue, by temporizing, or by resorting to the haunts of vulgarity and vice for support, it may be inferred with moral certainty that he is not a man of real respectability, nor is he entitled to public confidence. As a general rule, it may be affirmed that the man who *never intrigues* for office may be most safely *entrusted* with office; for the same noble qualities—his pride, or his integrity and sense of dignity—which make him disdain the mean arts of flattery and intrigue will restrain him from debasing himself by betraying his trust. Such a man cannot desire promotion unless he receives it from the respectable part of the community, for he considers no other promotion to be honorable.

Both in government and religion, form your opinions with deliberation, and when you have settled your opinions, adhere to them with firmness. Particularly would I commend to you this course in adopting your religious creed. And when you have attached yourself to any system from deliberate conviction, do not rashly and for light causes abandon it. When satisfied that you have embraced an error, conscience will direct you to renounce it. But let not a temporary inconvenience, a slight, or a fit of discontent for a trifling cause induce you to forsake the denomination with which you have been united. Such change evidences want of principle or want of firmness and stability, neither of which is compatible with true dignity of character.

"The Chief Glory of a Nation . . ."

From the Preface to *An American Dictionary of the English Language*, 1828

EDITOR'S COMMENTS

The completion of his greatest labor, *An American Dictionary of the English Language,* is described in Webster's own words: "I finished writing my Dictionary in January, 1825, at my lodgings in Cambridge, England. When I had come to the last word, I was seized with a trembling which made it somewhat difficult to hold my pen steady for writing. The cause seems to have been the thought that I might not then live to finish the work, or the thought that I was so near the end of my labors. But I summoned strength to finish the last word, and then walking about the room a few minutes I recovered."[1] Well might a man of seventy years tremble, from sheer exhaustion, after more than a quarter century of painstaking study and research and the laborious preparation *by hand* of almost seventy thousand word definitions.

When the dictionary appeared in 1828, the excellence of its definitions and etymologies overwhelmed the inevitable critics, and the bulky work won immediate and fulsome praise from many quarters. Unquestionably the best dictionary of its day, the work and its descendants have enjoyed such great acclaim that one may well speculate about the word "Webster" appearing one day in dictionaries to acknowledge the significance it already commands in popular usage. Immediately adopted as a standard by the Congress and the people of the United States, Webster's *An American Dictionary of the English Language* was soon —despite the hostility of insular critics—the standard in England itself. Thus did Webster perform singlehandedly a symbolic act of independence for America and fulfill in part his vision of America as a nation eminent in arts as in arms. The impact of this single work upon American culture may well have exceeded the aggregate effect of

[1] Ford, *Notes on the Life of Noah Webster,* II, 293.

Webster's many direct appeals for a heightened sense of cultural independence.

In many respects, the preface to Webster's monumental dictionary represents the man's matured nationalistic views. Absent are the "chimerical" radical enthusiasms of his youth and the acid overtones of his irascible disillusionment. The almost secure tone of this composition reflects Webster's recognition of the essential validity of his position and the ultimate worth of his lexicographic efforts. The obvious pride with which he cites evidence of an emerging American literature suggests that Webster felt at least a part of his vision of America had been achieved. Not completely devoid of the element of vanity that traces its way through Webster's career, nor free of his sense of self-sacrifice, the preface is nonetheless the temperate expression of a man who has achieved his biblical threescore and ten with the satisfaction of seeing the crowning effort of his life completed. It was the completion of this labor, combining his instinct for sober work with his desire to establish the cultural independence of American letters, that permitted him to go to his grave fifteen years later saying, "I'm ready to go; my work is all done . . ."[2]

[2] *Ibid.*, II, 367.

"*The Chief Glory of a Nation . . .*"

In the year 1783, just at the close of the revolution, I published an elementary book for facilitating the acquisition of our vernacular tongue and for correcting a vicious pronunciation which prevailed extensively among the common people of this country. Soon after the publication of that work, I believe in the following year, that learned and respectable scholar the Rev. Dr. Goodrich of Durham, one of the trustees of Yale College, suggested to me the propriety and expediency of my compiling a dictionary which should complete a system for the instruction of the citizens of this country in the language. At that time I could not indulge the thought, much less the hope, of undertaking such a work, as I was neither qualified by research, nor had I the means of support during the execution of the work, had I been disposed to undertake it. For many years, therefore, though I considered such a work as very desirable, yet it appeared to me impracticable, as I was under the necessity of devoting my time to other occupations for obtaining subsistence.

About twenty-seven years ago I began to think of attempting the compilation of a dictionary. I was induced to this undertaking not more by the suggestion of friends than by my own experience of the want of such a work while reading modern books of science. In this pursuit I found almost insuperable difficulties from the want of a dictionary for explaining many new words which recent discoveries in the physical sciences had introduced into use. To remedy this defect in part, I published my *Compendious Diction-*

ary in 1806, and soon after made preparations for undertaking a larger work.

My original design did not extend to an investigation of the origin and progress of language, much less of other languages. I limited my views to the correcting of certain errors in the best English dictionaries, and to the supplying of words in which they are deficient. But after writing through two letters of the alphabet, I determined to change my plan. I found myself embarrassed at every step for want of a knowledge of the origin of words which Johnson, Bailey, Junius, Skinner, and some other authors do not afford the means of obtaining. Then, laying aside my manuscripts and all books treating of language except lexicons and dictionaries, I endeavored, by a diligent comparison of words having the same or cognate radical letters in about twenty languages, to obtain a more correct knowledge of the primary sense of original words, of the affinities between the English and many other languages, and thus to enable myself to trace words to their source.

I had not pursued this course more than three or four years before I discovered that 'I had to unlearn a great deal that I had spent years in learning, and that it was necessary for me to go back to the first rudiments of a branch of erudition which I had before cultivated, as I had supposed, with success.

I spent ten years in this comparison of radical words and in forming a synopsis of the principal words in twenty languages, arranged in classes under their primary elements or letters. The result has been to open what are to me new views of language and to unfold what appear to be the genuine principles on which these languages are constructed.

After completing this synopsis, I proceeded to correct what I had written of the dictionary and to complete the remaining part of the work. But before I had finished it, I determined on a voyage to Europe, with the view of obtaining some books and some assistance which I wanted, of learning the real state of the pronunciation of our language in England as well as the general state of philology in that country, and of attempting to bring about some agreement of coincidence of opinions in regard to unsettled points in pronunciation and grammatical construction. In some of these objects I failed; in others my designs were answered.

It is not only important, but in a degree necessary, that the people of this country should have an *American Dictionary* of the English language; for, although the body of the language is the same as in England and it is desirable to perpetuate that sameness, yet some differences must exist. Language is the expression of ideas, and if the people of one country cannot preserve an identity of ideas, they cannot retain an identity of language. Now an identity of ideas depends materially upon a sameness of things or objects with which the people of the two countries are conversant. But in no two portions of the earth remote from each other can such identity be found. Even physical objects must be different. But the principal differences between the people of this country and of all others arise from different forms of government, different laws, institutions, and customs. Thus the practice of hawking and hunting, the institution of heraldry, and the feudal system of England originated terms which formed, and some of which now form, a necessary part of the language of that country; but in the United States many of these terms are no part of our present language—and they cannot be, for the things which they express do not exist in this country. They can be known to us only as obsolete or as foreign words. On the other hand, the institutions in this country which are new and peculiar give rise to new terms or to new applications of old terms unknown to the people of England, which cannot be explained by them and which will not be inserted in their dictionaries unless copied from ours. Thus the terms *land-office, land-warrant, location of land, consociation* of churches, *regent* of a university, *intendant* of a city, *plantation, selectmen, senate, congress, court, assembly, escheat,* &c., are either words not belonging to the language of England or they are applied to things in this country which do not exist in that. No person in this country will be satisfied with the English definitions of the words *congress, senate* and *assembly, court,* &c., for although these are words used in England, yet they are applied in this country to express ideas which they do not express in that country.

With our present constitutions of government, *escheat* can never have its feudal sense in the United States.

But this is not all. In many cases the nature of our government and of our civil institutions requires an appropriate language in the definition of words, even when the words express the same thing as in England. Thus the English dictionaries inform us that a *Justice* is one deputed by the *King* to do right by way of judgment—he is a *Lord* by his office, Justices of the Peace are appointed by the *King's commission*—language which is inaccurate in respect to this officer in the United States. So, *constitutionally* is defined by Todd or Chalmers *legally,* but in this country the distinction between *constitution* and *law* requires a different definition. In the United States a *plantation* is a very different thing from what it is in England. The word *marshal* in this country has one important application unknown in England or in Europe.

A great number of words in our language require to be defined in a phraseology accommodated to the condition and institutions of the people in these states, and the people of England must look to an American dictionary for a correct understanding of such terms.

The necessity, therefore, of a dictionary suited to the people of the United States is obvious; and I should suppose that, this fact being admitted, there could be no difference of opinion as to the *time* when such a work ought to be substituted for English dictionaries.

There are many other considerations of a public nature which serve to justify this attempt to furnish an American work which shall be a guide to the youth of the United States. Most of these are too obvious to require illustration.

One consideration, however, which is dictated by my own feelings, but which I trust will meet with approbation in correspondent feelings in my fellow citizens, ought not to be passed in silence. It is this. "The chief glory of a nation," says Dr. Johnson, "arises from its authors." With this opinion deeply impressed on my mind, I have the same ambition which actuated that great man when he expressed a wish to give celebrity to Bacon, to Hooker, to Milton, and to Boyle.

I do not, indeed, expect to add celebrity to the names of *Franklin, Washington, Adams, Jay, Madison, Marshall, Ramsay, Dwight, Smith, Trumbull, Hamilton, Belknap, Ames, Mason, Kent, Hare, Silliman, Cleaveland, Walsh, Irving*, and many other Americans distinguished by their writings or by their science; but it is with pride and satisfaction that I can place them as authorities on the same page with those of *Boyle, Hooker, Milton, Dryden, Addison, Ray, Milner, Cowper, Davy, Thomson*, and *Jameson*.

A life devoted to reading and to an investigation of the origin and principles of our vernacular language and especially a particular examination of the best English writers with a view to a comparison of their style and phraseology with those of the best American writers and with our colloquial usage, enables me to affirm with confidence that the genuine English idiom is as well preserved by the unmixed English of this country as it is by the best *English* writers. Examples to prove this fact will be found in the introduction to this work. It is true that many of our writers have neglected to cultivate taste and the embellishments of style, but even these have written the language in its genuine *idiom*. In this respect Franklin and Washington, whose language is their hereditary mother tongue unsophisticated by modern grammar, present as pure models of genuine English as Addison or Swift. But I may go farther and affirm with truth that our country has produced some of the best models of composition. The style of President Samuel S. Smith of Princeton, of the authors of the *Federalist*, of Mr. Ames, of Dr. Mason, of Mr. Harper, of Chancellor James Kent, the prose of Mr. Joel Barlow, of the legal decisions of the Supreme Court of the United States, of the reports of legal decisions in some of the particular states; and many other writings in purity, in elegance, and in technical precision, is equaled only by that of the best British authors and surpassed by that of no English compositions of a similar kind.

The United States commenced their existence under circumstances wholly novel and unexampled in the history of nations. They commenced with civilization, with learning, with science, with constitutions of free government, and with that best gift of

God to man, the Christian religion. Their population is now equal to that of England; in arts and sciences our citizens are very little behind the most enlightened people on earth—in some respects they have no superiors—and our language, within two centuries, will be spoken by more people in this country than any other language on earth except the Chinese in Asia, and even that may not be an exception.

It has been my aim in this work, now offered to my fellow citizens, to ascertain the true principles of the language in its orthography and structure, to purify it from some palpable errors, and reduce the number of its anomalies, thus giving it more regularity and consistency in its forms, both of words and sentences, and in this manner to furnish a standard of our vernacular tongue which we shall not be ashamed to bequeath to *three hundred millions of people* who are destined to occupy and, I hope, to adorn the vast territory within our jurisdiction.

If the language can be improved in regularity so as to be more easily acquired by our own citizens and by foreigners, and thus be rendered a more useful instrument for the propagation of science, arts, civilization, and Christianity; if it can be rescued from the mischievous influence of sciolists and that dabbling spirit of innovation which is perpetually disturbing its settled usages and filling it with anomalies; if, in short, our vernacular language can be redeemed from corruptions and our philology and literature from degradation; it would be a source of great satisfaction to me to be one among the instruments of promoting these valuable objects. If this object cannot be effected and my wishes and hopes are to be frustrated, my labor will be lost, and this work must sink into oblivion.

This dictionary, like all others of the kind, must be left in some degree imperfect; for what individual is competent to trace to their source and define in all their various applications—popular, scientific, and technical—*sixty* or *seventy thousand* words! It satisfies my mind that I have done all that my health, my talents, and my pecuniary means would enable me to accomplish. I present it to my fellow citizens, not with frigid indifference, but with my ardent wishes for their improvement and their happiness and for the continued increase of the wealth, the learning, the moral and religious elevation of character, and the glory of my country.

To that great and benevolent Being who during the preparation of this work has sustained a feeble constitution amidst obstacles and toils, disappointments, infirmities, and depression, who has twice borne me and my manuscripts in safety across the Atlantic and given me strength and resolution to bring the work to a close, I would present the tribute of my most grateful acknowledgments. And if the talent which he entrusted to my care has not been put to the most profitable use in his service, I hope it has not been "kept laid up in a napkin" and that any misapplication of it may be graciously forgiven.

AFTERWORD

The story of Noah Webster does not, of course, end with the publication of his great dictionary in 1828. The man himself lived on until 1843, and his work—especially the dictionary—continues to have a life of its own.

Noah Webster was seventy years old when his *An American Dictionary of the English Language* appeared in 1828, but he hardly paused to rest on his laurels. He continued to lead an active life—writing, revising, traveling to promote his books, and engaging in political controversy. Only a month before his death, on May 28, 1843, he had sent a collection of his papers to the press, and early that May he had finished correcting a new edition of his spelling book.

In the winter of 1830, Webster made a trip to Washington to support the new copyright bill then before Congress. He spent several months there and came away feeling partially responsible for the bill's passing both houses under the urging of his son-in-law William W. Ellsworth, Congressman from Connecticut, and Daniel Webster. While he was in Washington, Webster, characteristically, took care of other interests, too. By the time he returned to New Haven, he had managed to secure the endorsement of more than 100 members of both houses of Congress and the Judiciary for his whole series of books, from the speller to his most recent abridgment of the big dictionary.

In the 1830's, Webster was busy publishing and editing still more schoolbooks. Among these was his *Biography, for the Use of Schools* (1830), which contained thirty-seven short biographies of historical persons, from Homer to Cowper. He included the lives of seven scriptural figures, including Jesus, and, significantly, twenty-one Americans, including his own ancestor, Governor John Webster. The next year he brought out *The Elementary Primer*, a little book of thirty-six pages with many pictures of things that would be familiar to children, as well as several poems, one of which was the perennial "Twinkle, Twinkle, Little Star."

In 1832, Webster issued his *History of the United States,* which was intended for use in the schools. He had earlier introduced American history in a revision of the reader that made up Part III of *A Grammatical Institute of the English Language.* He had also, through the years, included sketches of American history in other books and pamphlets. Prefixed to his *History of the United States* was a "Brief Historical Account of Our Ancestors from the Dispersion at Babel to the Migration to America and of the Conquest of South America by the Spaniards."

In 1822, Webster had conceived the idea of revising the King James Bible. He firmly believed in the Bible as the repository of the revealed word of God, but he was concerned lest the antiquated language of 1611 confuse the contemporary reader instead of bringing him spiritual illumination. As Webster's preparation for his dictionary had shown him, some of the words and grammatical locutions of the 1611 Bible were no longer in use; as he says, concerning the necessity of clarifying the meaning of many Biblical passages:

> Whenever words are understood in a sense different from that which they had when introduced and different from that of the original languages, they do not present to the reader the *Word of God.* . . . A version of the scriptures for popular use should consist of words expressing the sense which is most common in popular usage, so that the *first ideas* suggested to the reader should be the true meaning of such words according to the original languages. . . . My principal aim is to remedy this evil.[1]

Webster also felt that some of the words in the Bible "fortify and extend infidelity." In keeping with the contemporary tendency toward euphemism, he set about correcting what seemed to be the objectionable and immoral language of the Bible. For the phrase "to give suck," Webster substituted "to nourish," for "teat" he used "breast," for "to go a-whoring" he used "to go astray," and in place of "womb" he used "stomach."

Webster saw that the Bible was the most widely read book in the land, and he related his revision of the Bible to his continuing support for a language indigenously American. "The language of the Scriptures ought to be pure, chaste, simple, and perspicuous, free from any words or phrases which may excite observation by their singularity, and neither debased by vulgarisms nor tricked out with the ornaments of affected elegance." Compared with more recent revisions, Webster's contained very few corrections. It is not clear whether he made too many or too few for his revision to have

---

[1] Quoted in Warfel, *Noah Webster: Schoolmaster to America,* pp. 406–7.

sold well; to the end of his life, however, he considered his revision of the Bible to be his most important work.

Webster's last years in New Haven were busy ones; he had at last achieved some of the honor his years of labor deserved. He entertained visitors from all over the world and was asked to make many public appearances. When President Andrew Jackson came to New Haven, Webster went to pay his respects, and so imposing and venerable was the appearance of this old New England schoolmaster that many other visitors, mistaking him for the President, asked to shake his hand. In 1840, at the age of eighty-two, he delivered a historical address on the occasion of the 200th anniversary of the founding of Connecticut. A local newspaper account of that event reported that he spoke for an hour and a half and that "his voice was so clear and distinct as to be heard from all parts of the Center Church."

But when the patriarch died in New Haven, at the age of eighty-five, another fascinating story was really just beginning—the story of the publishing history of Webster's two most successful works, the "Blue-Backed Speller," with which he had launched his publishing career, and the dictionary. That the story is still unfolding makes it all the more fascinating.

When Webster died, the rights to his spelling book were sold to a New York publishing firm. According to H. L. Mencken, "In the 1840's the publishers, George F. Cooledge & Bros., devoted the whole capacity of the fastest steam press in the United States to the printing of it. The press turned out 525 copies an hour, or 5,250 a day. It was constructed expressly for printing Webster's elementary spelling book . . . at an expense of $5,000."[2]

In 1857, the rights were bought by G. & C. Merriam of Springfield, Massachusetts, but they did not publish the book over their name, contracting instead with D. Appleton for publication. By this time, the speller was over seventy years old, but D. Appleton "took it up with as much enthusiasm as if it were the newest up-to-date manuscript."[3] And in 1880, when an interviewer asked him what his firm's best-selling book was, William H. Appleton replied, "Webster's speller, and it has the largest sale of any book in the world except the Bible. We sell a million copies a year. Yes, and we have been selling it at that rate for forty years. . . . We sell them in cases of seventy-two dozen, and they are bought by all the large dry-goods houses and supply stores, and furnished by them to every crossroads store."[4]

[2] H. L. Mencken, *The American Language* (New York: Alfred A. Knopf, 1936), p. 385.
[3] Mark Sullivan, *Our Times* (New York: Charles Scribner's Sons, 1927), II, 89.
[4] Quoted in Ervin C. Shoemaker, *Noah Webster: Pioneer of Learning* (New York: Columbia University Press, 1936), p. 89.

Though many of the spellings in Webster's books reflected his own Connecticut pronunciation—and he thought of New England speech as the purest English—his "Blue-Backed Speller" sold widely throughout the country. One of his account books lists the names of 100 publishers who had secured the rights of publication for various districts throughout the country. The first book printed west of the Rocky Mountains, in Oregon, in 1847, was Webster's speller. Although the South seceded from the Union, it found it could not do without Webster; in 1863, an Atlanta printer brought out an edition that followed the licensed copies of the late 1840's, with the fables omitted and Biblical verses added to give scriptural support to the institution of slavery. The editor of this edition remarked that "no better spelling-book than Dr. Webster's has ever been presented to the American people" and that he felt that he could not improve on it.[5] In addition, William Holmes McGuffey adopted Webster's spellings in his universally used readers, so that nearly every American child was exposed to Webster's spelling in one way or another. The Cherokee Indian Chief Sequoah used Webster's speller as a model when he committed the Cherokee language to writing. And in Japan, in 1871, it was used as the basis for a Japanese-English textbook, which was printed from wood blocks cut by hand.

As this is written, the American Book Company is still doing a lively business in selling a facsimile edition of the speller. It is unlikely that any printed book has ever sold more copies—the Bible excepted—than has Noah Webster's first literary effort, produced in 1783 when he was but twenty-five years old.

The publishing history of the great dictionary, if less impressive in a quantitative sense, is at least as dramatic. George Philip Krapp observed, "The American child passed by natural progression from the spelling book to the dictionary, but the dictionary he never outgrew."[6] And that dictionary has, for the most part, been one of the editions of Webster. The American edition of 1828, of which 2,500 copies were printed, did not sell rapidly, probably because the price was $20. In 1836, though, Webster advertised that the American edition had been exhausted and that orders would be filled with copies of the British edition (which had come out in installments from 1830 to 1832). Webster published a second edition in 1841, but most of the copies were still unsold and unbound at his death.[7]

---

[5] Quoted in Emily Ellsworth Ford Skeel and Edwin H. Carpenter (eds.), *A Bibliography of the Writings of Noah Webster* (New York: New York Public Library, 1958), p. 131.

[6] George Philip Krapp, *The English Language in America* (New York: The Century Co., 1925), I, 328.

[7] In 1829, Webster hired Joseph E. Worcester to do an abridgment of his *An American Dictionary of the English Language*, and he brought out another abridgment himself in 1830. In 1845, two years after his father's death, William Webster published *The Elementary School Dictionary*, based on the 1828 edition of *An American Dictionary the English Language*.

When Webster died in 1843, his heirs sold the unbound sheets of the 1841 edition to the firm of J. S. & C. Adams of Amherst, Massachusetts. But the Adams firm soon found that their purchase was more than they could carry. The dictionary, in two large volumes priced at $15, was too expensive to move well. They therefore offered all remaining sheets of the dictionary to G. & C. Merriam, who, as successful booksellers, might presumably know how to dispose of the white elephant. The Merriams closed the deal after arranging a simultaneous contract with the Webster heirs to insure their rights to public revisions, and so became the owners of Webster's *An American Dictionary of the English Language.*

The Merriams had been publishing and selling books in Springfield for more than forty years, but when they acquired the rights to the Webster dictionaries they decided to specialize in dictionaries and lawbooks. Despite his reverence for Yankee ingenuity and American enterprise, Webster was never a very good businessman,[8] but the Merriams were. The first thing they did was to undertake a new one-volume edition of the dictionary to sell for only $6, in contrast to the nearly prohibitive price of the 1828 edition. To do this, they employed as editor Webster's son-in-law Chauncey A. Goodrich, who was a Yale professor as well as Webster's literary executor. In addition, they engaged specialists from various fields to write and check specialized definitions; among the fields represented were ecclesiastical history, chemistry, mathematics, geology, astronomy, fine arts, and law. Engaging specialists for technical advice has become standard practice in American dictionary-making, but it was an innovation then. This new edition appeared in 1847 with no radical changes from the 1828 edition, except for the addition of some 15,000 words—the 1828 edition contained 70,000 entries, the 1847 edition 85,000. However, because of the lower price and the promotional efforts of the publishers, this was the first of the Webster dictionaries to reach a substantial market. The Merriams went on to print many varieties of Webster dictionaries, including abridgments and school dictionaries. Seeing the need for completely new editions at periodic intervals, the G. & C. Merriam Company published the *New Illustrated Royal* in 1864, the *International* in 1890, the *New International* in 1909, the *New International, Second Edition* in 1934, and the *Third New International* in 1961.

In 1830, Joseph E. Worcester, whom Webster had employed the previous year to edit an abridgment of the 1828 dictionary, brought out a dictionary of his own, *A Comprehensive Pronouncing and Explanatory Dictionary*, in which he denied accusations that he used Webster's material; and in 1846, Worcester published *A Universal and Critical Dictionary*, which was apparently designed to compete with Webster's big dictionary. When Worces-

---

[8] Bob Eddy, "The *Courant* Took a Chance," *The Quill*, LII, No. 5 (May, 1964).

ter published this last dictionary in Britain in 1853, however, it bore on its title page the statement, "Compiled from the Materials of Noah Webster, LL.D., by Joseph E. Worcester." This attempt to take advantage of Webster's favorable reputation in England, apparently without the consent of Worcester's American publishers, was just what the Merriams had been waiting for. They had been accusing Worcester's publishers of plagiarism for years, and now they had what they took to be proof. They published and widely distributed a pamphlet entitled "A Gross Literary Fraud Detected." Worcester's publishers answered with an equally acrimonious pamphlet, and the great "Dictionary War" was on.

Fought mostly with pamphlets and newspaper editorials, the controversy was taken up in state legislatures and academic halls. Harvard and the University of Virginia came out for Worcester, while Yale and most of the others backed Webster. Oliver Wendell Holmes commented wryly on the loyalties and extravagant advertising claims that the "Dictionary War" engendered, noting in his *Poet at the Breakfast Table* that a certain word was "considered vulgar by the nobility and gentry of the Mother Country, and it is not to be found in Mr. Worcester's Dictionary, on which, as is well known, the literary men of this metropolis [Boston] are by special statute allowed to be sworn in place of the Bible. I know one, certainly, who never takes his oath on any other dictionary, any advertising claims to the contrary notwithstanding."[9]

The hostilities were virtually over, though, when the Merriams published their 1864 Webster's *New Illustrated Royal*, which was in every respect the best English-language dictionary in the world. The Worcester books were not without merit, however, and offered the buyer a fairly clear choice—"Worcester standing on the whole closer to British use, and Webster, in some respects, standing for a local and somewhat provincial use."[10]

The Worcester adherents had to admit that, in spite of their efforts, Webster's usages had been adopted by *Harper's*, the most widely circulated monthly magazine, and by the best edited and most widely circulated newspaper in the United States, Horace Greeley's *New York Tribune*.

The Merriams fought a continuing battle to keep the name *Webster* as the company's private property, since they had bought the copyright to his *An American Dictionary of the English Language*. But the copyright on the name had expired with the first copyright on the dictionary, following which all sorts of dictionaries, good and bad, took up the name Webster because it ensured good sales. In 1917, the Merriam Company was partly successful in its court battle; a federal court ruled that, with certain

[9] Quoted in Krapp, *op. cit.*, I, 372.
[10] *Ibid.*

exceptions, other publishers who use the Webster name must print the following warning on their title page: "This dictionary is not published by the original publishers of Webster's *Dictionary* or by their successors." But, since most people do not look at the title pages of the books they buy and since the ruling does not discourage the use of small type, other publishers have been pretty well able to circumvent this difficulty.

Webster's dictionaries have enjoyed a degree of success far beyond what the modest sales of the 1828 dictionary promised. They have been adopted by the U.S. Congress, most state legislatures, and most courts of law. Even before the British edition came out in 1830–32, the British courts were beginning to cite the American edition. In 1831, a reviewer in *Colburn's New Monthly Magazine*, a respectable British publication, observed half seriously: "It is curious that the most important English dictionary, with the most profound and accurate investigation of the origin and principles of our native language published in the present day, would be produced by an American." Webster's dictionaries, in short, became standard in Britain as well as in America. In the first really new British dictionary since Samuel Johnson, *The Imperial Dictionary* by John Ogilvie, published in 1850, the preface acknowledged Webster as its basis and praised it as "superior to every other dictionary hitherto published."[11]

Given the publishing history of his "Blue-Backed Speller" and his "Great Dictionary," it can be no exaggeration to say, as his foremost biographer has said, that Noah Webster was "Schoolmaster to America." And, given the influence of his teachings, it can be stated with certainty that Webster taught an emphatic lesson on being American.

[11] Quoted in Shoemaker, *op. cit.*, p. 240.

A BIBLIOGRAPHICAL NOTE

Professor Harry R. Warfel is principally responsible for the preservation and promotion of the historical record of Noah Webster's life and accomplishments. His biography, *Noah Webster: Schoolmaster to America* (New York: The Macmillan Co., 1936), is the fullest to date, and his edition of the *Letters of Noah Webster* (New York: Library Publishers, 1953) is invaluable. Horace E. Scudder's biography, *Noah Webster* (Boston: Houghton Mifflin Co., 1881), was the first one undertaken, a part of the "American Men of Letters Series"; while Ervin C. Shoemaker's study, *Noah Webster: Pioneer of Learning* (New York: Columbia University Press, 1936), is more scholarly, if less sympathetic and less readable, than Warfel's.

Two Webster descendants have made important contributions to the record. Emily Ellsworth Ford Skeel has edited, together with Edwin H. Carpenter, *A Bibliography of the Writings of Noah Webster* (New York: New York Public Library, 1958); and Emily Ellsworth Fowler Ford has brought forth a two-volume collection of *Notes on the Life of Noah Webster*, edited by Emily Ellsworth Ford Skeel (New York: privately printed, 1912), which includes his diaries and correspondence.

For those who feel the need for a counterbalance to the sympathetic treatment of Webster by Warfel, several articles are recommended. Thomas Pyles' *Words and Ways of American English* (New York: Random House, 1952) contains two pertinent chapters: "Noah Webster, Man and Symbol," pp. 93–124, and "Linguistic Nationalism and the Schoolmaster," pp. 74–92. Charlton Laird's "Etymology, Anglo-Saxon and Noah Webster," *American Speech*, Vol. XXI (February, 1946), concludes that "to assume that Webster was more than a mediocre student of Anglo-Saxon is perhaps to accept his professions too credulously."

For essentially balanced views, the reader is referred to Edward Wagenknecht's "The Man Behind the Dictionary," *Virginia Quarterly Review*, Vol. V (April, 1929), and Kemp Malone's "A Linguistic Patriot," *American Speech*, Vol. I (October, 1925).

Webster's lexicographic work has, of course, been treated most fully. Among the most enlightening contributions on this score, in addition to the Pyles and Laird articles already mentioned, are George Philip Krapp's *The English Language in America* (2 vols.; New York: The Century Co., 1925), James R. Hulbert's *Dictionaries, British and American* (New York: Oxford University Press, 1955), Kenneth G. Wilson, R. H. Hendrickson, and Peter A. Taylor's *Harbrace Guide to Dictionaries* (New York: Harcourt, Brace & World, 1963), and Robert K. Leavitt's *Noah's Ark, New England Yankees, and the Endless Quest* (Springfield, Mass.: G. & C. Merriam Co., 1947). This last contains an account of the history of the G. & C. Merriam Company.